10 Things Parents Should Know About Drug & Alcohol Abuse

Intercourse, PA 17534

Design by Dawn J. Ranck

10 THINGS PARENTS SHOULD KNOW ABOUT DRUG AND ALCOHOL ABUSE

International Standard Book Number: 1-56148-013-4
Library of Congress Catalog Card Number: 91-70664

Library of Congress Cataloging-in-Publication Data

Hostetler, Jeptha R.
10 things parents should know about drug and alcohol abuse / Jep Hostetler.
p. cm.
Includes bibliographical references.
ISBN 1-56148-013-4
1. Drug abuse—United States. 2. Alcoholism—United States. 3. Youth—United States--Drug use. 4. Youth—United States—Alcohol use. 5. Drug abuse—United States—Prevention. 6. Alcoholism—United States—Prevention. I. Title. II. Title: Ten things parents should know about drug and alcohol abuse.
HV5825.H67 1991
649'.4—dc20 91-70664
CIP

Table of Contents

To Begin

It is tempting to believe that drugs have made a desert of our world. Not only does the problem of abuse grow ever larger, we non-users are inclined to surrender to what seems inevitable: the problem is bigger than we are. Furthermore, we are intimidated by our own lack of expertise in knowing how to work at prevention or treatment.

A wasteland does surround us. But I have come firmly to believe that it does not need to overtake us. In my circuit of speaking to gatherings of young people I encounter wistful, yet well couched calls for help. These are from materially secure youth who have some troubling unanswered questions and often a barely identified bothersome vacancy within. My proposals for parents and other interested adults grow out of those insightful, often disturbing, conversations with pre-teens, teenagers and young adults.

These are bite-sized ideas, but I believe they can help us begin foisting off this burdensome, even violent, emptiness that ends in drug abuse:

1. Get accurate answers to our questions (Chapter 1).
2. Debunk the myths (Chapter 2).
3. Do some solid groundwork at home (Chapter 3).
4. Make specific efforts in our own communities (Chapter 4).

We are not in a war against drugs. Drugs are drugs with no life of their own. They are immobile substances, promoted, perpetuated, sold and used by human beings, from young children to aging adults.

Our real war is against meaninglessness and against poverty of the soul. It is a war for the allegiance of our children. It is a war against the behavior of a society that glorifies rugged individualism and creates an unprecedented sense of isolation and loneliness for our young adults. We are doing battle to save our children from becoming "spoiled" and empty of meaning.

We are effective only to the extent that we have found meaning in our own lives. Furthermore, to help our children discover their own spiritual dimensions we must give them deliberate, focused attention over time.

Recent research about recovery from alcohol and drug dependence, as well as studies related to drug/alcohol prevention, points to the need for persons to possess spiritual awareness in order to build a solid base for not using alcohol and other drugs or to have complete recovery from their use. The spiritual nature of human beings cannot be ignored if we are to nurture whole and complete human development.

There are, however, no guarantees. Even as we do everything in our power to provide nurturing, proactive, freeing, disciplined settings for our children, some young people will make disappointing decisions. In fact, all children will make unwise choices, choices that disappoint their parents. Parents need to understand that they are not responsible for all of their childrens' poor decisions. Parents are often blamed or blame themselves for the woes of their children, creating untold guilt and shame.

This book is about avoiding panic when your children make a decision regarding alcohol and other drugs, that is different from what you taught them. This book is especially about doing the best you can and relaxing along the way.

Dr. Jep Hostetler
Faculty of Preventive Medicine
Ohio State University
Columbus, Ohio

10

Most Asked Questions About Drugs

QUESTION #1:

Our sixth grade daughter told us that two of her best friends are smoking marijuana and drinking beer. What should we do?

ANSWER:

This is a situation with multiple layers! Your first fear is likely that your daughter will be influenced to try the same drugs the others are using. It is true that adolescents who associate with drug-using peers are more likely to try drugs. So your first impulse is to find a way to stop your daughter from associating with the other girls. The second part of your concern has to do with how you might help the two girls change their behavior before they become attached to alcohol or marijuana.

Yes, there are things you can and should do. First of all, don't be rash. It would do little good to instantly forbid your daughter to see these friends.

You may be angry to know that there are drugs in your community and you may be disappointed that your daughter hangs out with girls who use drugs. Consider the fact that your daughter told you about the situation.

She could have kept it a secret. The fact that she told you indicates that she does not approve of the behavior, and that she probably expects you to do something about it. Commend your daughter for her honesty and concern.

One of the easiest things at this point is to do nothing further with the information your daughter has given you, quietly hoping it goes away. On the other hand, you could call the girls' parents and express your concern that alcohol and marijuana are present in the school, noting that your daughter has become aware of it as well. You may ask them if their daughters have talked about it at all. This plants a seed in the parents' minds that their daughters may have seen or heard about the drugs at school, but stops short of accusing their daughters of drug use.

You may want to contact the school and inquire about what they have learned about children using drugs. Unfortunately, the school may not be too helpful. Some school administrators are quite protective of their schools, finding it difficult to admit that there are drugs in their schools. However, your phone call will have alerted them to the situation. It is a rare school that does not have some form of drug problem.

QUESTION #2:

What is a drug?

ANSWER:

When we talk about drugs of abuse, we usually mean four kinds of drugs:

1. Illegal chemicals (substances) such as marijuana, cocaine, crack, speed, heroin, LSD and PCP are examples.

2. Alcohol. Often not considered a drug by adults, this drug is found in all alcoholic beverages—wine coolers, beer, vodka, whiskey, mixed drinks, rum and gin.

3. Tobacco products such as cigarettes, cigars, pipe tobacco, snuff and chewing tobacco. These products contain a variety of drugs. The most addicting compound in tobacco products is nicotine.

4. Prescription drugs. Even though these drugs are prescribed for medical purposes, they can be abused. Common prescription drugs include barbiturates, valium, insulin, some narcotics, tranquilizers and hundreds of others.

By the broadest definition, a drug is any substance that can be put into the body and which alters the natural state of the person consuming it. Drugs can be swallowed, injected, snorted, sniffed, smoked or placed under the skin with needles.

Drugs which affect the state of one's mind are called mood-altering or psychoactive drugs. Drugs that are most abused are those that change the mind, mood or manners of the user. The most highly sought after drugs are those that have a rapid effect and give the most pleasure, while at the same time have the least undesirable side effects.

In order for a drug to work it must enter the bloodstream where it is circulated throughout the body, eventually reaching the brain. In general, drugs of abuse can be further classified as follows:

• Uppers—These drugs stimulate the nervous system, including the brain and the central nervous system. They make the heart beat faster; the user feels a sense of energy, a pick-up. They increase one's blood pressure as well. Common examples of this kind of drug include nicotine, caffeine, amphetamines (speed), cocaine and crack.

•Downers (Depressants)—These drugs slow down the nervous system. They make the heart beat slower; the user feels a sense of relaxation. The most common example of this drug is ethyl alcohol, or beverage alcohol. Other examples of downers include barbiturates (barbs), sopors, Valium and Xanax.

• Narcotics—These drugs are noted for their ability to reduce pain because they effectively block pain sensations to the brain. One side effect of many of these drugs is a feeling of well-being or euphoria. Heroin is a prime example. Also included in this group are morphine, codeine, opium, Percodan, Dilaudid and several other synthetic narcotics.

•Hallucinogens—These drugs have the ability to make persons hallucinate or to see and hear strange things. They cause users to go on a "trip," which simply means that they experience changes in their senses. They may see, hear, taste and feel unusual and bizarre things, like melting colors, moving walls, peculiar sound patterns and an unusual perception of time. The most abused drug in this group is LSD. One could also put THC, the active ingredient in marijuana, in this class. Here, too, are mescaline and psilocybin, products from a special kind of cactus and certain mushrooms.

• Inhalants—These drugs are generally sniffed and are found in a liquid or gas form. They can cause a variety of reactions from dizziness and nausea to euphoria and excitement. This group includes volatile nitrites (like amyl nitrite), gasoline, some types of glue, White Out and paint thinner, just to name a few.

• PCP (Phencyclidine)—Also known as Peace Pill or Angel Dust, this drug is often put in a category by itself. It is an anesthetic-type drug that can have a variety of effects, from hallucinations to contracted skeletal muscles. It can cause violence and produce a short-lived and intense increase in strength.

Originally this drug was produced as an animal tranquilizer. It is no longer legal to manufacture PCP. It is taken by humans as an additive to tobacco or marijuana.

• Marijuana—This substance is a bit difficult to classify. One of its main actions is to act as a depressant, slowing down reflexes and relaxing the consumer. The most active ingredient in marijuana is THC, tetra-hydro-cannabinol. In high doses this drug can cause hallucinations. Even though marijuana can be eaten, it is more commonly smoked.

QUESTION #3:

How do children get into drugs?

ANSWER:

There are many starting places. Each child begins by making a choice. And that decision is never made in a vacuum.

To a greater or lesser extent, most children have used legal drugs from a young age. Most have eaten chocolate or have drunk cola beverages, coffee or tea, all of which can contain caffeine or caffeine-like substances. (For this reason, some religious groups abstain from the use of coffee, caffeinated tea, and soft drinks that contain caffeine.) The child's choice to use a drug, therefore, is not a completely new adventure.

Using an illegal drug, such as nicotine, alcohol or marijuana, usually starts in the presence of friends. The first illegal drug most children use is one of two drugs that are considered legal for adults—alcohol or tobacco products.

Experimenting with cigarettes, snuff, dip or chewing tobacco and/or beer or wine coolers is a common first step toward the continuing use of drugs. If the child's first experience with a drug is positive without negative effects, the child is likely to return to the drug. It worked! It produced a good feeling and there was apparently no harm done.

Since the drug worked so well, the young person makes a choice to do it again, with similar favorable results. In fact, this repeated use may lead to the young person looking for opportunities to use a given drug. He is actively pursuing the "mood swing" or good feeling the drug provided. With little immediate negative consequences from the use of the drug, the youngster may continue to use it more and more frequently.

Because of the addiction potential for many drugs, this repeated use can lead to harmful involvement with the drug. Drug use can now begin to bring some negative results. The young person may suffer from guilt and shame or may even lose control over when to use the drug or how much of the drug to use. She may begin to violate her own values and rules and develop schemes to insure that she can continue using the drug. Lying, stealing and cheating may become a part of this person's life.

Various forms of pain enter anyone's life who continues to use a drug. Pain can be from withdrawal from the use of the drug or from overdose of the drug. It may also be the pain of guilt. The only thing that seems to relieve this psychic or physical pain is more of the drug. The person has become truly drug-dependent and needs the drug just to feel normal.

The time it takes to go from the first use of a drug to

dependency on the drug hinges on three factors: 1) the type of drug, 2) the age of the user, and 3) the amount and frequency of use. In general, young people become dependent on drugs at a faster rate than do adults. Some drugs, such as crack, have a high addiction potential and can hook a user in a very short period of time. Nicotine is another drug with a fairly rapid addiction time.

QUESTION #4:

How do I know if my child is using drugs?
What do I look for?

ANSWER:

Drug use in its early stages is difficult to detect. Because drug use is illegal—including alcohol and tobacco—young people are going to hide their practice from their parents or other adults. Furthermore, different drugs produce varying signs and symptoms.

What to look for, then, is drug-taking behavior. To further confuse matters, some of these behaviors are normal as occasional adolescent conduct. However, a young person exhibiting several of the following characteristics, may be showing signs that he is using drugs:

- Becoming secretive or withdrawn
- Becoming unmotivated regarding things that previously caused excitement
- Change in friends
- Change in sleep patterns
- Red eyes (bloodshot from using marijuana)
- Graffiti (drug-oriented) on child's property

- Use of incense in the child's bedroom
- Becoming less concerned about personal appearance
- Wheezing, sneezing and coughing
- Depression
- Change in eating habits, often craving sweets
- Poor memory
- Flat affect and speech
- Money or other valuables are missing from the house
- Drug paraphernalia, rolling paper, pipes, etc. appear in child's bedroom
- Smell of alcohol on breath
- Coming home under the influence of "anything"
- Getting a lot of colds
- Truancy
- Smells like "burnt rope" (marijuana)

QUESTION #5

What is a gateway drug?

ANSWER:

Gateway refers to entering the world of illicit drug use. Research has shown that nearly all persons who have become drug-dependent can identify several drugs that they first used. With the exception of those who became drug-dependent due to prescription drugs, the majority of drug-dependent persons point to tobacco products and beverage alcohol as their first used drugs.

Children who sneak cigarettes or who steal their parents' alcohol are usually having their first illegal drug encounter. This does not necessarily mean that because they try cigarettes or other tobacco products, or, because they experiment with beer or wine coolers, they will progress to other drugs. It is true, however, that few drug-dependent persons started their addictive behavior using "hard" drugs such as heroin, crack or cocaine.

QUESTION #6:

We have discovered that our 14-year old son is using marijuana. What went wrong in our parenting?

ANSWER:

You may have done nothing wrong. You may be excellent parents, yet your child may make some poor choices.

Children try alcohol and other drugs for a variety of reasons. Recently the National Institute for Drug Abuse (NIDA) documented some of the major reasons:

1. Curiosity. Youngsters want to know what it feels like to be "high." The term "high," loosely interpreted, has several meanings: feeling good, feeling euphoric, feeling dreamy, experiencing altered states of consciousness, or simply feeling different from normal.

2. Excitement. Some researchers believe that it is normal to pursue altered states of consciousness. An example is the spinning that children often do to make themselves dizzy. Why do youngsters delight in playground merry-go-rounds? As children get older they try thrill rides at amusement parks. Even adults enjoy euphoric moments with great food, absorbing music, concerts, skiing, sexual activity and, of course, drinking alcoholic beverages and using licit or illicit drugs.

3. Peer Pressure. Usually children have their first cigarette or marijuana joint because friends offer it to them. Children do not perceive that as negative pressure, but rather as a positive way to belong to the group. Social fit is a powerful force and may nudge children and youth to try drugs.

4. Rebellion. Television commercials, magazine advertising, billboards, MTV, rock bands and former professional athletes all glamorize the use of mood-altering chemicals. Alcoholic beverages, particularly wine coolers and beer, are equated with "good times": "It doesn't get any better than this," "Let the good times roll," "The Silver Bullet doesn't slow you down," and "Head for the mountains" all portray the good life. Even though breweries are careful to use only adults in their television commercials, the actors are young looking and attractive.

Children and teenagers who want to be grown up try alcoholic beverages in the presence of friends who also want to be grown up. Using alcohol is one way a young person can defy adult rules. In fact, this behavior may not be so much a deliberate defiance of adult authority, as it is a way to prove that the young person is capable of making adult decisions.

5. Societal pressures. Material possessions and fashion statements have become the symbols of success in many segments of our society. Designer jeans, designer running shoes, gold chains, the right clothes, jewelry and hair styles, and being seen with the right people—all are part of the mystique of success. Young people are aware of the need to succeed, to look attractive, and to make a favorable impression. Drinking wine coolers, dipping snuff and smoking pot fit with some young persons' perceptions of what it means to be successful. Fortunately, smoking cigarettes is beginning to be less favorably regarded, so that more and more people are quitting or trying to quit. At the same time, many girls and young women are reveling in their freedom ("You've come a long way, baby") and are still choosing to smoke.

QUESTION #7:

How are children affected by their parents' use of drugs?

ANSWER:

It is no secret that children learn much from the habits, attitudes and behavior of their parents or significant other adults.

Research is conclusive that the majority of children mirror their parents when it comes to the use of alcohol and tobacco products. One government document announces, "The amount you drink or smoke is not the only behavior you show your children. They also notice why you drink or smoke, when you drink, and whether you drive, boat, swim, or perform any other activity that is dangerous when combined with alcohol." Scientific studies also indicate that children whose parents smoke are much more likely to become smokers themselves.

Even though research has not shown moderate drinking of alcoholic beverages in front of children to be harmful, adults who abstain from drinking have a better chance of having children who abstain from the use of alcohol.

A PROBLEM: Some parents who do not use alcohol or other drugs, including tobacco, sometimes make the mistake of not discussing alcohol or tobacco use with their children. Too often these parents assume that their children know where they stand and, therefore, will not use alcohol or tobacco products. These parents may not realize that children have many other adult role models affecting their choices.

QUESTION #8:

How shall I talk about alcohol and other drugs with my children?

ANSWER:

Thoughtfully, early and consistently!

Some of us believe that as long as our children do not bring up the subject, our situation is relatively safe and problem free.

Others of us fall into lecturing or scolding and making strong statements about what we will do if we ever catch our children using drugs.

A PROPOSAL: It is more productive to discuss alcohol and other drugs in a relaxed manner, over time, than to have a marathon lecture that shuts out any possibility of discussion. Begin talking about television programs, commercials, billboards, and magazine and radio advertising with your children when they are two and three years of age. Help them to learn some of the myths behind the ads and to understand the nature of the "good life" without the use of alcohol and other drugs. These discussions can turn into regular events as your child progresses through school. Critically evaluating advertising is a good tool to let your children know how you feel about drugs.

Research indicates that, in addition to family or other adult role models, children form many of their ideas about drug use from television and movies. Alcohol use and abuse are commonly portrayed in the electronic media, often without showing any negative consequences. Children's perception of alcohol use may be incorrect. Parents can dispel some of the misunderstandings if they are willing to talk about the issues surrounding alcohol and other drug use.

Many educators refer to "teachable moments" when a child is most receptive to learning. Don't miss them in regards to drug use. Many adolescents see movies in which a person under the influence of alcohol does dangerous things, like driving a car, with apparently no harmful effects to himself or other people. He always manages to come out of a drunken situation with a smile on his face and a chuckle. When you see such scenes with your children, capitalize on the natural opportunity to discuss the myths portrayed in the movie.

Share the facts with your children. Point out that in real life there are nondrinkers and nonsmokers who are attractive and talented. Give examples of how alcohol and other drugs dull one's judgment and muscle control and do not solve any problems. Ask your children what they think about the stars of stage, screen, music and sports who use alcohol and drugs. Listen! Try to understand your child's view. Acknowledge the validity of her ideas that have merit and counteract those that do not have any basis in fact.

Most of all, be consistent. It is difficult to have a discussion about alcohol and other drugs if you have a martini in one hand and a cigarette in the other. Drug use is drug use. If you want to make a statement you need to show you are able to moderate your own intake of alcohol and tobacco and refrain from the use of other harmful drugs.

QUESTION #9:

There seem to be many drug prevention programs. Are any of them effective?

ANSWER:

There are three levels of prevention related to the use of alcohol and other drugs.

The first is Primary Prevention. Its goal is to promote healthy lifestyles and, in turn, prevent people from using any harmful substances at all. For example, it is highly unlikely that a five-year-old boy will have smoked a cigarette. Primary prevention aims to reinforce his decision not to use tobacco products. Primary prevention strengthens positive attitudes toward taking care of oneself and negative attitudes toward the use of any harmful substances.

Secondary Prevention works to stop the progression of any health-defeating behaviors once they have started: for example, helping adolescents to stop smoking. Secondary prevention is aimed at encouraging people to quit unhealthful habits and begin a lifestyle that is health-promoting. Technically, any prevention program that targets an adult population is secondary prevention, since the opportunity for well defined primary prevention is past.

Tertiary Prevention has the goal of preventing death, even if the process of drug dependency has advanced to a detrimental level. An example is intervening to help an addicted person enter a treatment program. Even though tertiary prevention is not treatment, it does promote the resources of treatment facilities. Tertiary prevention is aimed at saving lives, even those that have been devastated by chronic drug and alcohol abuse.

High quality prevention efforts incorporate all three levels of prevention. Primary prevention, wedded with solid educational efforts, should happen from kindergarten through high school. Here is where we indoctrinate our children with the benefits of living healthy lives and taking care of themselves.

If primary prevention accomplished what we ideally intend, secondary prevention would not be necessary. However, in the real world, some children try smoking cigarettes or sneak alcoholic beverages from their parents' stock of alcohol. Secondary prevention is aimed at letting these children know that they are not bad. Rather, they have made choices that will have negative consequences and they can quit the use of harmful substances. Secondary prevention emphasizes that *now* is the time to discontinue using drugs, before you become drug-dependent.

Tertiary prevention is usually not strongly emphasized in prevention programs since it moves into the treatment mode. Most prevention programs simply are not geared for treatment efforts and thus are not capable of handling this level of prevention.

QUESTION #10:

We feel helpless and alone in battling drug abuse. Is there anything we can do to help our community fight this epidemic?

ANSWER:

Yes! (This is a resounding yes!)

Two major blocks stand in the way of community action: community denial and fear of involvement. The easiest thing to do is to do nothing. But unless individuals begin to shoulder some responsibility we will never win the battle against drug abuse.

It is essential that communities—through the efforts of individual citizens—acknowledge that they have a problem with alcohol and other drugs. You can begin by taking a look at arrest records. How many young people are being arrested for Driving Under the Influence of alcohol or other drugs?

What do high school students do at their parties on weekends? Does anyone in the community talk about what is happening? Are there facts to be found to indicate the extent of the problem? (See the chapter, "10 Things You

Can Do in Your Community," page 98, for specific suggestions about how to become involved.)

The other blockade to community intervention is fear. Some parents fear that if their own children use or begin to use drugs, they will appear hypocritical if they are active against drug use. Perhaps more honestly, some parents fear getting involved because they do not want to look like prohibitionists. We cherish independence and are convinced that we can work things out by ourselves. But attacking a community drug abuse problem will never be successful if it is attempted in single households. Each of us must reach out beyond the confines of our own homes, despite our family's struggles, to make community prevention work.

10

Myths About Drugs

MYTH #1:

If parents would only teach their children right from wrong we would not have all this teenage drug abuse.

FACT:

Knowing right from wrong does not automatically prevent a child from experimenting with alcohol and other drugs.

The reasoning goes like this: if we could get parents to teach morals so that children knew right from wrong, children would choose right most of the time. Such reasoning simplifies the blame—parents. The logic assumes that if young people have enough information about drugs and are well enough informed about the dangers of drugs, they will not try them.

✦

Connie was a "good girl" all through elementary school and high school. Everyone knew that her religious upbringing and her family's strict rules gave her a clear sense of right and wrong. Connie's entrance into the large state university opened her eyes to new ways of thinking and behaving. She promised her parents she would stay out of trouble, and they were confident that she would continue to be a model daughter.

Connie's new way of thinking and acting included weekly trips to the local bars, where she gained entrance by using a fake identification card. Connie loved to dance. Adding alcohol to the scene seemed to pick up her spirits and give her a new sense of freedom.

Soon Connie began to smoke cigarettes. Her weekly trips to local pubs turned into nightly rounds of beer-drinking. She was becoming more and more attached to the lift that alcohol gave her. Her work started to slip and she began to miss classes. Her roommates were concerned about her, but could do little to stop her from indulging in alcohol. It was not until Connie had an automobile crash, while under the influence of alcohol, that her parents became aware of her drinking problem.

Recent basic prevention research documents a fact that may be disappointing: strong educational efforts promoting knowledge about the harmful effects of alcohol and other drugs do little to affect an adolescent's choice about whether or not to use drugs. *Information alone does not deter a young person from using drugs.* However, information coupled with a broad-spectrum program—one that has the people of the community and its organizations involved in the building of self-esteem, peer counseling, problem solving skill training, and so on—is the strongest approach to prevention.

Conscientious parents are concerned with teaching right from wrong. The difficulty comes, of course, with distinguishing the degrees of right and wrong. For example, if a parent uses alcohol moderately and enjoys drinking alcohol at home as well as at parties, it is unlikely that this parent will see drinking in a totally negative light. When a son or daughter takes a drink the parent does not see it as wrong. Other parents who abstain from using alcohol are likely to regard drinking, in any form, as wrong or even sinful.

✦

Connie had to drop out of college in order to help pay for the damages from her car accident. In addition, she was now so attached to alcohol that she could not complete her studies. She needed professional help. Her parents, both solid, church-going people, were embarrassed and ashamed of what had become of their daughter. They prayed that she would turn her life around. Since they were teetotalers, that is, abstainers, they were angry and sad that Connie had taken even one drink. They saw their lives as failures because of Connie's involvement with alcohol, not to mention the fact that she was also addicted to cigarettes.

✦

It is true that persons who regularly attend religious

gatherings are less likely to use drugs. Research shows that one of the high-risk factors is a person's lack of regular attendance at any religious event. Teaching right from wrong in association with formal religious training is one method for reducing the risk of a child's using drugs, even though in Connie's case she made choices to go in a different direction.

One's early decisions to first use drugs and alcohol may bring the guilt that any anti-value behavior brings. Even though Connie knew "right from wrong," once she made the decision to use alcohol she discovered that it did something special for her. She was willing to live with the guilt and soon found herself trapped by the natural history of alcoholism and drug dependence which includes the progression of the disease.

For many reasons some people react differently to alcohol than the general population. This was true for Connie. For such persons especially, once the process is started it is difficult to quit, even though these individuals may know that they are making wrong decisions. The insidious nature of the process is such that as the person decides to use the drug of choice again and again, she becomes nearly incapable of making the decision not to use it.

Connie concealed her drinking and smoking from her parents until a crisis brought it to light. She carried double guilt—from hiding her behavior, as well as going against her parents' values and her own values.

Clearly, teaching a child right from wrong is morally correct and should be promoted in all segments of society, but less than rigorous teaching in this area is not the sole cause of adolescent drug problems. It is one factor that may contribute to the problem.

MYTH #2:

When I was a teenager we did not have all these drugs that they have today.

FACT:

Drugs have been readily available for each generation. It is true that the variety of drugs available today is greater than a generation ago.

Sounds like a parent speaking! While some of today's drugs were not available to past generations, alcohol and tobacco products were within easy reach. These products are the top drug killers in our society today. Illicit drugs, including marijuana, crack, cocaine, speed and heroin, are responsible for approximately 7,000 drug-related deaths per year in the United States. Alcohol and tobacco are responsible for over 325,000 premature deaths per year in the United States.

This myth fosters the idea that our drug abuse problems are caused by an increase in the types and amounts of available drugs. True, the more accessible a drug, the more use it will tend to have. But the multiplying numbers of drugs is not the single cause of increased adolescent drug abuse. It may be one factor in the mix of causes.

✦

Jeff was only eight when he heard about corncob pipes. Living on a farm, Jeff found it easy to design and make the pipes. He cut off a corncob, dug out the center and inserted a hollow willow stick. No one had bothered to tell Jeff that corn silk must be dried before it can be smoked. His several attempts at lighting the green corn silk met with negative results. Looking for other combustible material, Jeff decided to use toilet tissue, briefly inhaling the smoke directly into his lungs. This proved to be a very uncomfortable experience, so Jeff disposed of the corncob pipe over the old orchard fence behind the barn.

✦

Many children and adolescents will try some kind of drugs. Parents may or may not be aware of their experimentation. Jeff was intrigued with smoking a pipe. He felt no direct peer pressure and no one was actually present when he made his ill-fated attempt. Other young people sample alcohol from their parents' liquor cabinet when Mom and Dad are out for the evening.

The point is, many young people are going to try the drugs that are available to them. Certainly there are new drugs from which to choose, including those in parents' medicine cabinets. But the heart of the matter is what motivates a young person to use drugs. Neither more drugs nor newer drugs can be cited as the sole reason for drug abuse in our society.

Admittedly, some of the newer drugs have strong dependency potential; they are highly addictive. Cocaine and crack are notable for their high addiction potential. The unfortunate reality is that when young people experiment with these two drugs they are in great danger of becoming addicted.

As a society, our insatiable appetite for mood-altering drugs continues to drive our drug use behavior. That, coupled with the large sums of money that can be made from selling drugs, creates a real force in the direction of drug use. Add to this mix the addictive nature of many drugs and we have a potent formula for continuing drug abuse.

MYTH #3:

It's heavy metal rock music and MTV that causes all this drug abuse among our teenagers.

FACT:

Some heavy metal rock music has lyrics that promote violence, sexual domination, drug use, masochism and sadism. But these words matched with music cannot be blamed alone for drug abuse.

Hard rock music is the cause of drug abuse, declare many parents. Their underlying assumption is that if we could just prevent our children from being exposed to hard rock music and MTV they would not turn to drugs. It is another version of the blame game. Simple. Direct.

There can be no doubt that some hard rock music, some MTV and some rap groups present music and lyrics that are inappropriate for adults to see and hear, let alone children. However, to single out these forms of entertainment as the chief cause of drug abuse is neither justified nor accurate.

✦

Charlie loves music. Without his Walkman he would be lost, or so it seems. When he was 11 years old he discovered the captivating world of rock music. At first it was the strong drum beat and the rhythm of the music that intrigued him. At age 13 he was introduced to AC/DC and discovered a whole new universe of sounds and beats. His parents became concerned because he spent a lot of time with his ears plugged into the music as he lay on his bed with the door closed.

When asked why he listens to "that" kind of music, he simply explains that it is the rhythm and the beat that interest him. He really does not care about the words, even though he knows them all (and his parents cannot understand most of them). The cassette printout reveals some rather obnoxious wording and suggestions. Certainly, the parents reason, this music must contribute to the drug use among our teenage population. They decide to destroy the cassettes and C.D.s and forbid Charlie, who is now 15, to listen to hard rock music any more.

Many hard rock stars and many young people who associate with them openly promote the use of marijuana, alcohol and other drugs. Some go so far as to encourage the use of cocaine and hallucinogens in their songs. Can this be the cause of runaway drug abuse in our society? No. Not by itself. It certainly is a contributing factor for those youngsters who saturate themselves with music that relentlessly endorses hedonism, instant gratification and the use of drugs to escape the realities of life. They cannot help but be influenced by the messages.

Even though an adolescent's fascination with hard rock music, MTV and rap music, in and of itself, probably does not cause drug use and abuse, it can be one of the signs that your young person is making choices that expose him or her to a more open subculture, one that indeed does foster the use of drugs. Parents face difficult decisions regarding the kind of music their children listen to. How much is too much when it comes to drug- and violence-laced lyrics? What about going to rock concerts? Is it harmful for adolescents to be exposed to the rock stars that produce the music?

The answers to these questions are related to moderation. Compare it to a food diet. If one consumes junk food and has a diet loaded with fats and cholesterol, that person's health will be adversely affected. If young people have a steady diet of heavy metal rock music and are glued to MTV at every opportunity, it is fairly clear that most of their role models are not astronauts, scientists, missionaries, teachers or merchants.

Understandably, there are degrees of danger. Is a steady diet of so-called light rock music any better than hard rock music? How much is too much? Where do we draw the line? The bottom line has to do with moderation and balance.

Listening to heavy metal rock music and watching occasional MTV is not going to turn your son or daughter into a dope fiend. However, caution should be the order of the day. A steady diet of music with questionable values contributes to the making of a person with uncertain values, with or without drugs. Many young people, having listened to rock music for several years, tire of the banging, thumping and screeching, and their tastes change. They do grow up. They do not seem to be drug-users any more than the general population.

MYTH #4:

There are good drugs and bad drugs.

FACT:

Drugs are drugs. Some drugs have a more adverse effect on the body and mind than do others, but drugs are chemical compounds with no "goodness" or "badness" inherent in their structures.

A 42-year-old father of two teenagers is discussing the problem of drug abuse among the younger population. His obvious anger and resentment regarding "all those bad drugs out there" has culminated in a lengthy tirade about pushers and pimps and all the other evil elements in our society. As he makes these statements he lights his sixth cigarette in the past two hours and downs his third martini.

✦

Have you noticed that drugs are labeled good or bad according to who is doing the labeling and what drugs that person uses? Example: many reasonably healthy persons use caffeine, a drug. Since it is relatively harmless it is considered a good drug. Many adults use alcohol with no negative consequences. Besides, the drug—alcohol—is legal. Therefore, it is a good drug in many people's eyes. Drugs are usually labeled bad only if they are illegal and if they bring crime and violence with them.

✦

A serious middle ear infection caused Melanie's temperature to rise to a dangerous level. Eight-month-old children are often susceptible to these kinds of infections. A quick trip to the pediatrician resulted in a prescription for antibiotics and medication to reduce fever. Within hours her fever was reduced, and within 24 hours the infection was beginning to subside. Penicillin brought about the abatement of the infection.

✦

Three questions can help us determine a drug's potential for good or ill. First, is it legal? Second, how was it obtained? Third, how is it used?

Properly prescribed and used medications are a boon to our health. They bring relief and healing to otherwise ailing people.

Legal drugs, such as alcohol and tobacco products, create more ambivalence. Over 85 percent of the adult population who enjoy good wine or an occasional beer or mixed drink do not see alcohol as a bad drug. It becomes bad only when it is mixed with driving or when drunken behavior leads to abuse or other violence. Most alcohol users do not see themselves as abusive or violent, and most are not. That attitude carries over to our feelings about adolescent alcohol use. Statements such as, "Thank goodness my son only drinks beer; I'm sure glad he's not into drugs," are heard at all levels of our society. The fallacy here is the belief that alcohol is not a drug.

Smoking cigarettes is more and more taboo in our society. A generation ago a young man would wander into a drug store and state with some bravado, "Give me a pack of smokes," and then in a whisper, "Where are the condoms?" Today you are more likely to hear, "Give me a pack of condoms," and then in subdued tones, "And I'll also have a pack of Lights." We are becoming sharply aware of the irrefutable evidence that cigarette-smoking is hazardous to our hearts, lungs, circulation and overall health. Few would argue that tobacco products are good drugs.

Drugs are compounds which when taken can cause good or bad effects on the body. Most of us believe that correctly used medicine is helpful, but if that same medicine is overused or abused it becomes a bad drug. The drug has not changed. The point is that nearly anything we can consume has potential for good or bad effects on the body. Overeating, for example, is the excessive use of food. As a society we declare some drugs illegal because of the danger involved in consuming them.

MYTH #5:

Kids take drugs today because they have never learned to work.

FACT:

Whether or not one knows how to work has little bearing on whether one becomes a drug-user.

More high school youth are working at part-time jobs than ever before in the history of our country. Young people with cash have the opportunity to buy the things they want. With more money to spend, and more options on which to spend it, working teenagers are a prime target for drug sales, including alcohol.

The implication in this myth seems to be that if teenagers were taught responsibility through work, they would value their time and therefore value their own health. Consequently, hard-working youth would not do drugs. Scientific literature does not suggest that hard-working youth shy away from drugs. There is evidence to suggest that young people who give indications of being responsible are more resistant to drug use. Simply learning to work is not a guarantee that a young person will stay off drugs.

MYTH #6:

I do not know anyone who is addicted to drugs.

FACT:

Unless you live as a recluse, isolated from civilization, you interact with many persons who are addicted to drugs. You know them; you simply do not know of their addiction.

Only three to five percent of the persons with alcoholism are of the skid-row level. The majority of persons with alcoholism are functioning, to a greater or lesser degree, in our society. They are teachers, doctors, lawyers, truck drivers, janitors and builders, just to name a few. They are also our children. It is estimated that several million youth under the age of 18 years are already dependent on one or more drugs. Many of these young people are closet addicts, with few persons being aware of their addiction.

✦

Jerry did not start smoking until he finished college and began graduate school. He was able to confine his smoking to the outdoors or to situations where there was plenty of ventilation. He often found himself in restrooms and behind buildings where he would sneak cigarettes. Today he always carries a toothbrush and an assortment of breath mints and breath fresheners. If you were to ask some of Jerry's closest friends whether or not he smokes they would be nearly unanimous that Jerry is a non-smoker.

✦

If you know a smoker, you know an addicted person. If you know someone that simply must have his cup of coffee in the morning, as well as five or six cups during the day, you know an addicted person. Our society's general attitude toward coffee addiction and, to a lesser degree, nicotine addiction is one of tolerance. We do not regard these people as drug addicts. We still imagine addicts as down-and-out bums on the street.

Nearly everyone knows a person that is addicted to one or more drugs. Our failure to see these habits as drug addiction is a further index to what we as a society will tolerate. The very fact that we have difficulty identifying persons addicted to drugs, if the drugs are considered acceptable, reveals much about our attitudes toward drugs.

MYTH #7:

It's the schools' fault that we have all this teenage drug abuse.

FACT:

Drug abuse is a system-wide problem. Schools, churches and families all play roles in prevention or the lack of organized prevention programs.

Schools do play a major role in our children's lives, and they can have quality or weak drug-use prevention programs. To blame the schools categorically, however, is as unproductive as blaming the churches or blaming parents. The fact remains that until an entire community refuses to tolerate drug use little can be done to stop the problem. We keep seeking a scapegoat to blame for alcohol and other drug use in our communities.

It would be a better use of our collective energy to develop prevention programs involving each of the major sectors of a community.

Myth #8:

If children have good self-esteem they will not do drugs.

Fact:

Good self-esteem does not prevent the use of alcohol among the adolescent population.

The good news is that building self-esteem in our children is one of the better ways to build an armament against drug use. The bad news is that the drug of choice, even for those with solid self-esteem who choose to use drugs, is usually alcohol.

The reality is that there is not one factor alone that will prevent drug use and abuse among our children. Solid prevention efforts must involve, by design, an array of tactics and approaches. Building self-esteem is one, among several, of the better approaches to primary prevention.

MYTH #9:

Poverty causes drug abuse.

FACT:

Drug abuse is not limited to any social class, nor is poverty a sole cause of drug abuse.

NEWS FLASH: *"The local narcotics squad has just confiscated 14 ounces of cocaine at an east-side crack house. Details to follow!"* As you glance up at the television you see three young men, spread-eagled on the floor, as agents strap their wrists together with plastic bands. The room is in disarray and the arrested men are poorly dressed. The myth is reinforced: poverty causes drug abuse.

Drug abuse among our adolescent population is no respecter of class, wealth, culture or ethnic grouping. Some drugs are more prevalent among certain cultures, but the net effect is that poverty alone does not create drug abuse. It is true that selling and distributing illicit drugs brings immense wealth to a few people for a period of time. (Some mistakenly believe that drug-selling is a viable way to escape poverty on a permanent basis. For a rare individual this financial escape hatch may work out for a time). It is also a fact that drug use is a contributing cause to the increase in poverty in a community. Young people turn to drugs when their lives seem hopeless and helpless, and the poverty-drug-use-poverty spiral gains momentum.

✦

Sandy works hard for a living. He has to help his mother and his three sisters find enough money to pay the rent and supply food for their single-parent household. Sandy sells cocaine—not crack cocaine—just street cocaine. As soon as he gets home from school he makes his connection and picks up 30 to 50 grams of cocaine. Today it is selling for $80 a gram, and if things go well he can sell all the cocaine by 6 p.m. For every gram he sells he can make four dollars. If he works hard he can sell up to 50 grams in one evening. Profit for the night—$200. It beats working at the burger joint down the road. The only problem is that Sandy has to watch out for the police and protect himself from other dealers, not to mention the chance of getting beaten up by someone who just wants to take his money.

To whom does he sell it? Primarily to middle and upper middle class clients who drive by his corner every evening. He sells a few grams to local regulars, but his main clients are middle class, upstanding citizens. It is not unusual to have buyers that pick up five or six grams at a time, always on a cash only basis. No names are exchanged, only cocaine and cash.

Sandy is likely to eventually get busted and find himself in the detention center. His term will be relatively short because it will be his first offense and he is a minor. Back out on the streets, Sandy will be in business once again. Sandy is 15 years old.

✦

This is a fairly common scenario, but not the only way that cocaine and crack are distributed. How else do drugs get to middle class America?

People from the "burbs" are some of Sandy's buyers. These drugs find their way into the hands of adolescent users who happen to go to school where your children attend. At this level, it is the invitation of a trusted friend that gives your child her first encounter with cocaine. It really does not matter whether you live in the most affluent neighborhood or the poorest one, children are introduced to illicit drugs, from marijuana to cocaine, by their friends. The mythical man in a raincoat, hovering at a corner of the school yard, selling drugs to kids, is a rarity. Rich children and poor children alike obtain drugs from friends.

It is not material poverty alone that causes drug abuse. It may be, more accurately, poverty in terms of meaning in life that leads to drug use and abuse.

MYTH #10:

All young people are going to try drugs, but they will grow out of it.

FACT:

Not all young people are going to try drugs and, of those who do, nearly ten percent will not grow out of it.

This myth is partially true. Some young people who try drugs are fortunate enough to escape the clutches of the particular drugs they used. This is particularly true with alcohol. Only about ten percent of the drinking population will become alcohol abusers or persons with alcoholism. The fact remains that certain drugs are much more dependency producing than is alcohol. Crack, cocaine, nicotine, heroin and particularly the narcotics are all drugs that people have a very difficult time outgrowing. These drugs are powerful reinforcers. The more a person takes, the more he or she wants to go back to the original feeling.

Did you ever attend a church picnic during which

several of the men took a short break to go for a walk in the woods? Everyone knew that Fred and John were on a smoke break. Why did these men have to go off to the woods? They were addicted to one of the most dependency producing drugs known to human beings. In fact, persons who smoke behave similarly to those who are addicted to cocaine. They may return from a break with the sniffles, talking faster, acting a bit hyper, and, in certain cases, becoming somewhat obnoxious.

The list of drugs that have high addiction potential is long. To suggest that all young people who experiment with drugs will grow out of the behavior is simply a misconception and a false hope. Some will never make it out of the trap. The progressive nature of drug dependency makes it difficult to predict just who will be able to grow out of their use of chemicals.

Although treatment may offer an escape, it is not the same as outgrowing the use of drugs. It is, instead, a matter of learning a new lifestyle. A person must choose to remove herself from the cues that first got her started using drugs.

Some researchers liken alcoholism or drug dependency to illnesses like diabetes. Although there are no known cures for either one, both are chronic, treatable diseases from which people can recover and lead relatively normal lives. Approximately ten percent of those young people who choose to use alcohol or other drugs will show signs of the disease of alcoholism or chemical dependency.

10

Things You Can Do in Your Home

1. Teach Values

Like it or not, we teach values to our children almost automatically. For better or worse, children learn their values from what they see us do and say. We can choose to move from teaching values by osmosis to actively talking about why we do what we do. It is a natural yet often overlooked step because we assume our children simply know our values.

When you see ads on television, on billboards and in magazines, notice the societal values they embody. Talk about what you observe with your children and let them know your views. When your values are in conflict with societal norms, explain why. Your children likely have a general idea about how you stand on issues, but if you discuss these matters with them, you give them the opportunity to reflect on their own feelings and values.

When you see the frontier man on a billboard sporting a cigarette, see it as a moment to comment on what the advertiser is trying to portray. Point out to your children how death-dealing, nicotine-promoting companies attempt to make smoking cigarettes look glamorous or macho. Do they know why you have chosen not to smoke or dip snuff or chew tobacco?

When you see violence, use the occasion to talk about other options for settling disagreements. Encourage the use of words instead of weapons.

✦

A five-year-old boy was watching the news with his parents and the commentator showed clips of graphic fighting and violence. The young boy asked, "Why don't they use their words?" In his school the teachers were emphasizing the importance of "using your words" instead of hitting, pushing, shoving, biting and spitting. Values.

✦

Recent research about the presence of alcohol on television programs indicates that only a few prime-time shows completely exclude the use of alcohol. Most have drinking episodes or show a character offering a hospitality drink. When we see these acceptable societal norms on television, we have a golden opportunity to talk with our children about our own values.

These discussions regarding our feelings about alcohol and other drugs are most successful if we conduct them in a relaxed atmosphere, before our children are ever confronted with decisions about their own use of these substances. Make an effort to avoid overstating your case and becoming defensive. Certainly drugs can be and are often very harmful. However, not everyone who uses alcohol will become an alcoholic. Make sure your stance is objective and honest. Children soon learn that we are exaggerating when we promote stories that imply that anyone who ever touches alcohol will become an alcoholic, or when we fabricate horror tales to enhance our positions, or overemphasize the bizarre and ugly true cases that actually happen. The important point is to clearly state our own values and to live as consistently as we can in regard to those values.

Truth-telling can be fostered if we hold the same criteria for ourselves as we demand from our children. When honesty is upheld as a concrete, unwavering value, then children should not be punished for telling the truth. We may be saddened or shocked by what they say, but we can assure our children that we will always love them even though we are disappointed with what they have done. We may need to enforce consequences for decisions they have made that are against our values, while at the same time assuring our children that we really do care about them and will continue to love them.

2. Teach Sharing and Altruism

Self-centeredness is one cause of self-abuse, whether a person uses drugs, alcohol or food.

We often hear self-centered children referred to as "spoiled," "brats" or "selfish." What is it about these children that elicits these negative words? While the answer may be complex, these children's behavior patterns often carry a common thread: selfishness.

We can teach altruism and sharing to our children. It is true that newborns are incapable of understanding the world beyond getting their needs met: being fed, and kept safe, dry and warm. But as infants are socialized they learn about other people and other people's rights, wants and needs. This process requires years. Some children learn inadequately. Others do not learn at all.

Our society reveres symbols of success and gives support to getting all you can out of life. Our advertising promotes the good life and consumptive lifestyles. We vigorously pursue things. Children reared in this environment learn the expectations of such a society. Parents are part of the societal picture and easily become seduced by the greed that surrounds them. In order to teach altruism and sharing principles, we parents must deliberately combat the insidious forces fueling our own consumptive lifestyles.

Children can learn altruism, or consideration and respect for others, at an early age, if it is modeled for them. They can become giving persons by copying their parents in giving roles. They will learn giving styles and giving methods as they observe their parents' attitudes toward and respect for others.

Altruism has to do with how we view other people and our relationships to them. For example, with a bit of forethought, we parents can include our children in those events that help or support others. Our children can be part of selecting a gift for a birthday, graduation or anniversary. They can co-sign greeting or get-well cards. Better still, they can make cards for others, not to solicit praise, but to express interest in other persons' well-being. Talk about why you send cards and why you think it is important to think about others.

Start early to help young ones send thank-you notes for the generosity others have shown toward them. We can help children create habits of gratefulness if we show them the way and encourage them to participate when we send our own thank-you notes.

Joyce has a rather unusual calendar in her kitchen. It looks like an ordinary calendar, with the appropriate picture for each month displayed on the top half and the dates in the squares on the bottom half. At the beginning of each calendar year Joyce takes time to write, in red, birthdays, anniversaries and other important dates on each month's page. Each day, despite her busy schedule, Joyce glances at the calendar, looking several days ahead to see who should be getting a card. Joyce's consistent, steady practice of sending cards brightens the days of her countless friends and relatives.

✦

It is not surprising that Joyce's children are acquiring a generous and thoughtful attitude. It is not surprising that her children are involved in sending their own cards and notes to various people in their church, school and community.

Are you a cookie-baker? To whom do you give the cookies? Do your children understand why you go to the bother of making special cookies and why you give them away? Are you a neighborhood handy person? When you fix the neighbor's sink, do your children know why you are doing it? Do you encourage them to be helpful in their own way? When a youngster is slightly injured with a scrape on the knee or a bump on the elbow, can you show the kind of concern that reflects a genuine interest in others?

These are simple attitudes in action, values being lived out. It is admirable that a parent takes time to show a caring and sharing attitude; it is even better if the parent takes a few moments to include the child in carrying out the activities and explains the thinking behind the action. Our attitudes towards others are keenly observed and mimicked by our children.

✦

Sarah has been a first grade teacher for nearly thirty years. In a recent news interview she expressed her sadness over an increase in violence, even among first grade students, as the front-line solution to conflicts. In Sarah's estimation, violence is now the first option for settling differences in the schoolyard or quarrels over possessions. Many of the children she teaches seem to have no impulse to first talk about conflicts they encounter.

✦

Can children learn nonviolence? Yes, if we take time to demonstrate nonviolent options, as well as talk with them about the violence present in our society. Begin by teaching and modeling respect for all persons, regardless of race, color, creed or political ideology. Respect includes refusing to put down any nationality, church, political group or race and discovering with our children the richness that comes from understanding the wonderful variety of cultures and populations. Do you attend multi-cultural events? Do you take your children with you? We display our attitudes toward others in the way we regard their art, history, music and theater, in the way we talk about these cultural gifts. Our children will mirror our attitudes toward other human beings.

Children also are quite aware of how we use our homes. Do we invite persons from other cultures, other faiths, other colors, to participate in our meals, our celebrations, our special events? Nonviolence includes having an open attitude toward all persons, whether it be in our homes or at events where we meet other cultures. We can open the world to our children in a way that helps them broaden their views and become more accepting of persons different from them.

Sharing is another part of altruism. All of us are possessive. Our natural instinct is to protect what we have and to keep things for ourselves. Sharing, then, must be learned—the attitude as well as the complex of behaviors. Sharing begins with a child thinking beyond her boundaries, becoming alert to other people's needs. She begins to sense when others are hurting and can give herself to support those needs.

Obviously, giving, in order to be effective, must be done with a willing attitude. Reluctant giving is not giving; it is a patronizing and demeaning exercise in self-righteousness. No matter how great our effort to teach our children about giving to others, we fail if we have negative attitudes about the giving. Children are cannily alert to our true feelings.

The next time you go to a convalescent home to visit an elderly member of your community or family, take your older children along with you. (It is not wise to take young children who may have colds or other communicable diseases.) Take children with you when you spend Christmas day serving meals at the community soup kitchen. Take them with you when you spend an afternoon with a Little Sister or a Little Brother. Take them along when you deliver a hot meal to a recovering neighbor. Have them help you in designing posters, cards or fresh flower arrangements you will be giving to others. Have them help you package goodies for a special college student or a friend that is in the penitentiary. Enlist their help when you put together a special birthday event for another child.

Simply put, show them the way to altruism and sharing. Show them the way to understanding others. Allow them to see and hear your attitudes as you give to others. They are willing and eager learners. Tell them your own stories. Tell them about the times people gave to you both in tangible and intangible ways, and how it made you feel.

What does all this have to do with drug abuse? What does it have to do with lowering the risk factors against one's future use of alcohol or other drugs? By teaching our children attitudes of benevolence, sharing and nurturing, as well as unselfish behavior, we are giving them meaning and a sense of belonging to the larger community. A sharing and caring attitude is a strong antidote to selfishness. Inasmuch as self-centeredness is one of the risk factors leading to the use of alcohol and other drugs, altruism and a keen awareness of the needs of others are firm building blocks in the process of giving our children meaning.

3. Do Things Together

Do you remember the first time you rode a sled down a snow-covered hill? Who was with you? Was there an adult in the picture? Do you remember the first time you peeled an orange all by yourself? Was there an adult around? Did you ever go fishing as a child? Who helped you put the bait on the hook? Do you remember the first book you read all by yourself? Who was by your shoulder giving you encouragement? Who taught you how to ride a bicycle? Do you remember a special adult that paid attention to you? He showed up at your school plays. She was at your graduation and at your wedding. Do any of these memories, after all these years, bring back warm feelings?

We are creating these special moments for our children. What they will remember as adults will probably not be those things we most believed would impress them. What they will remember are those occasions when Mom or Dad or another adult took time to include them in an activity. They will remember an event when Mom and Dad made a special effort to single them out, to choose to be with them.

✦

"Let's have a little adventure," Dad said, as he invited Oldest Daughter to be the first in line. "It's a special adventure, just for one daughter at a time," he went on.

Within a few minutes Dad had loaded one girl into a coaster wagon, along with some old newspaper, sticks and small boards, a pack of marshmallows and matches. It was only a ten-minute wagon ride to the back of the property. There they parked the wagon and unloaded the newspaper and wood. Between the two of them, they managed to get a small fire started. As the fire burned Dad invited Daughter to sit beside him on the wagon. They would tell stories, he said, that's what they would do. Soon the fire was ready for roasting the marshmallows. When the fire burned down, the adventure was nearly over and they returned to the house. The whole event took less than one hour. Another night, another daughter would have the special wagon ride. Almost forgotten by the father, "wagon adventure" is still remembered by his adult daughters.

✦

Our fast paced lives continually threaten to crowd out what we claim as our most significant possessions—our children. While we know they need us now, we regularly allow a week, perhaps two, even a month to go by without sitting down to hear what is happening in their lives.

Being present with our children is probably the most effective way to let them know we care for them. And one of the most energizing ways to do that is to play with them. There can never be too many horsey back rides, marbles, dominoes, Candy Land or other games that seem beneath an adult. Do you go down the sliding board with your children? Do you swing with them? Do you play hide and seek?

All of us remember our children begging us to play with them while we thought of ways to postpone or circumvent their particular requests, hoping they would find someone else to play with. Others of us have steered our children toward the television in order to continue doing what we want to do. Two hours slip by, then two days, two more weeks and we wonder where the time went and how our children grew up so fast. It may be helpful to reflect on what we have to do that is so important that we cannot regularly take several quality minutes to focus on our children's play.

If we mean to include our children in our lives (even learning to play with them), we will have to deliberately choose to be with them. It will not happen automatically.

Doing things together with our children is more than being physically near them. It means that we are present, that we choose to be there, and that, for the most part, we are having a good time. Like reluctant giving, reluctant playing is quickly seen as a sham by our children. When we do include them, and when we do decide to play with them, it will be all the more meaningful for all of us if we do it with vigor and gusto.

4. Develop a Sense of Humor

Being a parent is serious business, and it is easy to take it too seriously. We read the books, we obtain the advice of trusted friends, and we fear that our children will somehow not turn out the way we want. In the pursuit of perfect parenting, we can lose our sense of humor, if we ever had one. With the multiple responsibilities parents have, it can seem frivolous at times to have a good laugh.

Recent research indicates that laughter is not only a pleasure, but it also enhances the body's ability to ward off diseases. Laughter helps to reduce one's stress level. People who have the ability to laugh, and laugh heartily, are healthier, with a chance of recovering more quickly from illnesses, than humorless people. In addition, people with a sense of humor are more self-assured. They have more confidence in themselves than humorless folks. Healthy humor is the capacity to laugh at one's self and to laugh with others, while at the same time refraining from laughing *at* others.

Children do say funny things. Laugh about their capers, as long as you are not demeaning or showing a lack of respect toward your child. Laugh with other parents as you trade these stories.

More importantly, laugh with your children. Share

comic strips in the newspaper, laugh together as you watch cartoons, tell jokes and riddles to involve your children in developing and expressing their senses of humor. Write down stories about them that you are certain you will never forget, because you will forget many of them. Take time to remember them when you are driving or waiting. Have a good chuckle about your children's antics. Most of all, help your children to see that you are not perfect, that you do some rather hilarious things from time to time.

Encourage your children to enjoy laughter so they become free to share their joy. Then they will not be afraid to laugh at appropriate times; they will not be inhibited in expressing their senses of humor. A highly desirable trait in an employee, a friend, a spouse is a good sense of humor.

Examine your own sense of humor. Do you laugh easily? Can you laugh heartily? Are you too reserved to let go with a good belly laugh? Children know instinctively how to laugh. Watch them. Let them teach you. Encourage them in this marvelous expression of joy. Each new stage of development brings its own set of humorous situations. Stay attuned to them and learn to laugh with each new phase.

A genuine appreciation of humor is one of the earliest casualties to drug and alcohol abuse. Partying and drinking with friends can produce some "good times," and people will remember the exhilarating things that happened at last night's get-together. But it is hilarity tinged with darkness. Furthermore, when the drug/alcohol abuser is alone, his sense of humor vanishes. Crack and cocaine users become anhedonic; that is, they lose the ability to enjoy the simple pleasures of life. The high that crack brings makes formerly enjoyable natural highs pale by comparison.

If we can teach our children to enjoy the richness of the moment and to enjoy the laughter and humor that surrounds them, we are building character that has no need for chemical highs. Giving our children the gift of understanding and appreciating humor is yet another solid plank in the prevention platform.

5. Give Responsibility

At a recent conference in Ohio for high-risk youth, someone asked, "Why are so many adolescents turning to drugs?" The nearly 150 youth in attendance were asked to ponder the question and answer it as honestly as they could. There were some predictable answers, but the most frequently offered one caught many adults by surprise: "We want meaning in our lives!" The theme of the discussion that followed was, "Give us adults who care about children."

A few young people suggested stricter drug laws; some proposed more recreation centers and educational efforts; a handful supported organized drug-prevention programs. What the overwhelming majority asked for, however, was a feeling of belonging, of being seen as worthwhile contributors to society, of being taken seriously.

To feel that one belongs one must have a sense of worth and believe that one's presence in the community is important. That sense of responsibility begins to be developed at home.

You are the parent. This is your apartment, room or home. You are not running a hotel nor are you running a resort. You can foster a sense of community in your household when you ask each member to take charge of certain duties and expect each to carry out the tasks at hand.

Start early. Even little children can do little jobs. They can perform these tasks on a regular basis. Obviously they cannot be held as accountable as a 15-year-old, but they can have particular assignments that foster their accepting of responsibility. Depending on their physical development, many children can begin helping around the house as early as two or three years of age. There is no shortage of tasks they can perform, from putting away their toys to hanging up the dish towels.

Any person—child or adult—can accept responsibility if it is clear what the job is. The person in charge may need to demonstrate the particular task, probably several times, then reinforce the doer's positive movement in the direction of completing the task successfully. The same procedures involved in toilet training a small child, that is, rewards and encouragement for each small step in the process, can be used to involve young children in household chores. Obviously one needs to take into consideration children's varying attention spans and the possibility that they may genuinely forget a certain task.

The important concept here is to start giving responsibility early, so the child feels a sense of belonging and a sense of accomplishment. As the child heads off to school and progresses through the elementary years, increase her tasks and chores to meet her age level.

✦

Charlene has two teenage daughters and an eight-year-old son. Her employment outside the home is rigorous and demanding. Nevertheless she manages to prepare meals, clean the house and wash clothes for the family. On any given afternoon after school you can find her thirteen- and fifteen-year-old daughters lounging in chairs, chatting on the phone or listening to music in their rooms. Neither girl has ever used the washing machine. Charlene believes that a mother should provide the comforts for her children, which include preparing meals, washing clothes, folding clothes and cleaning house. Her son is playing a video game. At times the children complain about being bored.

✦

It does little good to require responsibility in your children if there is no consistency in your expectations. If it is all right to let the chores slide or to postpone the deadlines on a repeated basis, there is little reason to believe the children are learning responsibility. In fact, they are learning irresponsibility.

✦

Jill is ten. Once a week it is her job to make sure the small hall closet is in order. Along with the task goes the stipulation that she must be finished by 6 p.m. Friday evening or she may not use the telephone, watch television or listen to the radio or stereo. At 5:45 p.m. on Friday evening, Jill approaches her father, flashing her lovely brown eyes, pleading her case for an extension until noon Saturday for completing the task of cleaning the closet. Her father begins to give in, not wanting to upset his daughter, when Mother arrives. With clarity of purpose she reiterates that Jill must finish the project before she may have any of the privileges. Dad agrees. Following a brief round of tears Jill cleans the closet and the music begins.

✦

Learning responsibility has yet another angle: to experience the consequences of one's decisions. It is helpful to allow children to make choices and then let them live with the consequences of their decisions, as long as the results are not harmful to themselves or others. Purple hair is not a disease.

✦

Brothers Ron and Dan, ages ten and eleven, each received two dollars from Uncle Clyde at Christmastime. The brothers' parents dropped them off at the variety store and gave them permission to spend their money in any way they chose, with only one stipulation: that twenty cents be saved out to give to someone else. Dan bought several candy bars, a small bag of potato chips and a soda. Ron bought a pack of gum and a small set of screwdrivers. Dan soon saw the shortsightedness of his decision: Ron still had his screwdrivers and all he had was a stomachache.

✦

We do our children no favors if we continually rescue them from the consequences of their behavior. Discomfort and small amounts of psychic pain as direct results of one's decisions and irresponsibility are good teachers. Allow your children to learn from their experiences and encourage them to make wiser decisions in the future.

To balance a child's learning of responsibility, parents need to guard against overscheduling the child's life. We have dreams for our children; we want them to become healthy and responsible adults. Too easily we fall into the trap of living our lives through our children. Piano lessons, soccer, dance lessons, Girl Scouts, Boy Scouts, gymnastics, art lessons, church, camp, clubs, cheerleading—the list is nearly endless. While we give them increasing responsibility, we must allow time for children to be children. They do need time to play, time to be creative, to read and talk and explore. Our task, then, is to balance their helping with household tasks and other responsibilities with time for them to simply be children.

A child who is given tasks and responsibilities as a part of the household team has a sense of belonging to a family, a community, something bigger and fuller than being an isolated individual with few roots or ties. Faced with making decisions about drugs, children who feel a part of a larger community draw upon that experience in their moments of choice. Children's decisions surrounding drug use are flavored by their sense of belonging to a group that cares what they do.

6. Start With Yourself

Perhaps the most difficult task facing parents is to be good role models. We want to be good parents but our major training has been simply our own experiences of growing up. We attempt to mimic those good parenting techniques our parents used and we try to avoid the techniques we disliked. Why are we surprised when we find ourselves repeating some of the very things we found objectionable in our own parents? We are their offspring, and it is difficult to break free from their patterns of parenting unless we take an honest and objective inventory of our own approach to life. In the ideal world we would have time to analyze our past experiences and think through how we are going to bring up our own children. We do obtain advice from many sides, from Aunt Millie to the pastor at the church. There are a myriad of books on the subject of parenting, but it becomes overwhelming to sort through the wisdom of the experts. How much information can one parent absorb, sift out and use?

Start with yourself. Take a serious look at your own behaviors, even if it seems that you do not have time, that you have too many things to do. If you are serious about helping your children stay drug-free, you cannot afford not to take a good look at your own patterns of behavior in regards to several key issues:

1. Your Own Use of Drugs.

Are you a smoker? Nicotine is one of the most addictive drugs known to human beings. Chances are that had you known what you now know about smoking you never would have started. It is true that children who take up smoking are much more likely to do so if they have a parent or parents who smoke. So the question is, "Am I willing to give up smoking in order to become a good role model for my children?"

Women who smoke during pregnancy have a tendency to have babies of lower birth weight. Is this something you can accept? In addition, it is now clear that secondhand smoke has a negative affect on the health of babies and young children. Children who live in a home where there is smoking are more prone to have respiratory disorders, asthma, colds and bronchitis.

So, without necessarily condemning yourself for smoking, simply ask yourself the question, "Am I willing to give up smoking for the long-term gain of giving my children better health?" This question applies to fathers and mothers alike. Check the free smoking cessation programs in your area, including the American Lung Association and the American Cancer Society. Take that first step toward becoming the example you want to be for your children.

✦

Tom began smoking when he was seventeen years old. All through his college years he was a one-pack-a-day smoker. Early in his marriage he made a commitment to stop smoking as soon as he became a parent. The first child arrived and Tom adjusted his promise: he would stop smoking when the child reached one year of age. When his first child turned five Tom lost his father at age sixty-three to lung cancer and emphysema. Tom finally gave up smoking.

✦

Granted, it is a tough commitment to give up smoking. But if you really want to raise drug-free children, stopping smoking is one way to begin the process.

Do you drink alcoholic beverages? Consider your relationship to alcohol. Is it an important everyday drug to which you are really attached? Could you go more than three days without any use of it? Do you use alcohol in moderation, at special occasions or in a ritualistic manner?

The key is to determine the importance of alcohol in your life. If you are an abstainer, do you know why you abstain? Can you explain this position to your children? If you are a user, can you identify the reasons why you use it? If your children explained their rationale for using alcohol as you do (discounting for a moment the fact that it is illegal for them), would you accept those reasons?

The fact that you may be an abstainer is not, in and of itself, insurance that your children will be the same. It is true that children who are brought up in homes where alcohol is not used are less likely to use alcohol themselves.

CAUTION: Being an iron-fisted teetotaler, condemning all use of alcohol and swearing that your children will never drink the "devil's brew," will not provide your children with helpful views of alcohol. On the other hand, if you are a teetotaler and are clear about your values related to alcohol, as well as your reasons for not using it, your children have a better chance of assuming your values.

In our society the use of alcohol has become the norm, not only for adults but also for young adults. We are a drug-taking society. Thus, the decision not to use alcohol becomes difficult because it is going against convention. Non-drinkers are the ones that must defend their position, as opposed to drinkers! Choosing not to use alcohol tells your children clearly, "We will not support the alcohol beverage industry."

Before you have children, decide what you are going to do with alcohol. The reality is, our children experience peer and societal pressure to become alcohol-using people.

What other drugs do you use? Are you willing to take a complete inventory? All of this leads to a basic question: Do I want my children to learn drug-taking behavior from me? Children are mimics of the adults closest to them. The inconsistency of doing one thing and advocating the opposite is obvious. Children quickly recognize the double standard.

2. Eating Habits, Exercise and Stress Management.

Our children sense how well we are. They observe—and copy–our eating and exercise patterns. They know if we sit in front of the TV and munch our way through three hours of programming. They are clear about whether we take time to exercise on a regular basis. Ask them how you manage stress. They know. If you are serious about being a good example for your children, these are issues to work on. Numerous books and community programs can help you. You might ask an interested friend to help you structure your self-discipline, as well.

Prevention begins with you, the parent. If you really want to be effective in raising drug-free children, there are few alternatives to doing an inventory of the items listed above, and then making a deliberate choice to work on those areas in which you are the weakest. Modeling is the strongest prevention tool we know. Children learn by what they see.

These suggestions for good health apply at all times but especially during pregnancy and following delivery of the baby. One important caveat: Do not drink alcoholic beverages in any amount while pregnant. The National Institute for Alcohol Abuse and Alcoholism recommends total abstinence from the use of alcohol during an entire pregnancy.

You may say, "I do not smoke, I use no alcoholic beverages or drugs, I eat right and I exercise regularly, but I am still worried about my children getting into drugs." Congratulations on your healthy lifestyle. You are being a good role model. Your concern for drug use is justifiable because even though you are a good example, numerous other factors influence your child's choices. We will look at them in the following pages.

7. Agree on the Rules

All homes have certain expectations. Most have rules. These standards come from each spouse's home; they are the rules each learned while growing up. When a child enters the family these expectations tend to become more apparent. Sometimes the rules of both parents mesh and there is little tension over the assumptions behind the rules. On the other hand, there may be a great deal of conflict over the standards, both spoken and unspoken.

Rules are those principles and practical guidelines about how the household will be run. They can range from not coming to the table unless your hair is combed to not having the television on during meals. Rules can be as general as forbidding lying, cheating or stealing, or as specific as expecting a youngster to call home if there is any change in plans.

Some households are run on a battery of rules, many of which are strict, unreasonable and rather tedious. Other households have general guidelines that form a blanket over the conduct of both parents and children. One such guideline may be that no one in the house may invade the physical space of another person without that other person's permission. Practically, this means that there will be no hitting, spitting or shoving. It also means that if someone has the door to his room closed, it is necessary to knock on the door to obtain permission to enter. These rules apply to both children and parents alike. Children will not enter the parents' room without knocking, and parents will not enter the children's rooms without permission.

Rules have to do with acceptable and unacceptable behavior, not with tasks and chores.

Ideally parents should try to identify their individual expectations, discuss them and work out any necessary compromises regarding their implementation. It is impossible to predict all the situations where rules will be applied. However, as each new situation arises it is important that parents agree to be united in the rules they present to their children.

Examples of Household Rules:

–There will be no cursing in this house.
–There will be no lying, cheating or stealing.
–We will respect the other person's space by asking permission to enter each other's rooms.
–We will wash our faces and brush our teeth every morning.
–We will eat breakfast together.
–We will use no drugs other than doctor-prescribed medications.
–We will limit our telephone conversations to a certain number of minutes.
–We will not borrow each other's clothes without permission.

Some of these are basic principles reflecting fundamental values: the forbidding of lying, cheating or stealing, for example. Other rules spell out more specifically behavior that upholds foundational understandings: "We will eat breakfast together" shows the value we place on family togetherness.

Needless to say, these rules apply to the parents as well as the children. For a parent to condemn cheating, while at the same time driving 70 miles per hour in a 55 mph zone, gives the children a mixed message: "It is O.K. to cheat on some things."

Broken rules should not be treated as life-threatening. It should be clear, however, that consequences for breaking the rules will be enforced, not with severe physical punishment, but with sanctions that apply to whomever is guilty. Remember, you are the parent. If a child is to be in bed at a given time, then that time should be consistent, with lights out at the time you feel will give your children adequate sleep. In the same way, rules regarding drug use can be clearly stated and enforced. The key to how well any rules work depends upon how well you as a parent are abiding by the rules you have set for your children.

✦

Jim and Sue decided that their children should have a sliding scale for bed times. At age ten, the time was to be 9 p.m. When the children reached junior high school level, the bedtime hour was extended to 9:30 p.m. and when they reached the ninth grade bedtime was extended to 10 p.m. As they moved through high school the bedtime was negotiated with each adolescent, based on the individual's need for sleep. Exceptions were made for special situations and for weekends. Nevertheless, the rules were known by both children and parents, and there were consequences for infractions. For every half hour over the limit, the next evening's bedtime was made that much earlier.

✦

Rules can be hard to keep. However, households with a set of well defined rules create an atmosphere where respect for the rules and authority are quite evident. If you seriously attempt to acknowledge rules and put them in place, your children understand that they are not living in a vacuum, that the world does not revolve around them and that they are a part of a social group that cares enough to give them solid guidelines.

As children get older, rules can and should be negotiated by talking about them. We parents can fall into the trap of making rules and enforcing them without any input from our children. This is not to say that children should run the household. Instead, sometimes our rules are truly unreasonable (perhaps we have not updated them as our children have grown older) and we need to hear our children's feelings regarding them. As an example, it seems unfair to ground a child for three months for failing to clean the closet by 6 p.m. Friday evening.

The consequences for breaking rules are most effective if they focus on those things that are important to children. It does little good to design consequences that do not infringe on their activities. Taking away television time from a child that rarely watches television, or sentencing a child to her room where she has access to a television or a portable radio would be pointless. To be effective, consequences for breaking the rules must be meaningful to the child.

8. Learn to Listen

Children of all ages are more likely to turn to parents who are capable of listening, than to those who simply have all the answers. Listening is more than the absence of not talking. You may think you do have the right answer, and you want to make certain that your children know how you feel about a given subject. Nonetheless, it is important to hear what your child is really saying before offering your definitive answer to a troublesome situation. Listening takes concentration and practice.

Listening is part of the age-old admonition to maintain open lines of communication with your children. Consider the possibility that you are in a position to take charge of the listening, not the talking. If you take charge of the listening you will begin to understand what your children truly are trying to communicate to you.

There are many ways to approach listening. Here are seven suggestions that may help you listen to your children.

1. Mirror Listening

You can restate what your child has told you to show that you are trying to understand. Rephrasing your child's statements serves three purposes: it shows her that you are hearing what she is saying, it gives her time to hear, in your words, what she is saying and to consider her own feelings about it, and it assures her that you really do understand what she is saying.

2. Watching

Watch your children as they speak to you. What are they saying with their facial expressions and their bodies? When a child tells you that he is not sad, while at the same time you notice a trembling chin or eyes that are too bright, his facial and body language are trying to tell you the truth. If there is a discrepancy between the body language and what the child is telling you, believe the body language.

✦

Jimmy came home after school with a packet of caps for his cap pistol. He had no money to buy caps at the store just one block from school, yet somehow he had the caps. His older brother began to quiz Jimmy about where he got the caps. Jimmy first answered that he found them in several different locations. Then Jimmy's mother arrived and proceeded with the same line of questioning. As she continued, Jimmy's face began to show signs of impending tears even though his words were saying, "I got them from a friend."

✦

3. Encourage and Support

As an adult, haven't you found it easier to talk when you are with someone who encourages you and shows interest in what you are saying? Children respond positively to that same kind of support. When they are talking to you, smile, give them an encouraging nod or a small "I see" or even a hug. Sometimes simply reaching for your child's hand is the encouragement he needs to continue talking.

When a parent's body language and facial expressions display anger or boredom or disappointment, it is difficult for the child to say what is on her mind. Encouragement and support also includes being nonjudgmental as your child tries to tell you his version of the truth.

4. Use Encouraging Phrases

In addition to a knowing nod or a touch on the hand, encouraging phrases help your child to go on speaking. Use phrases that best suit you, such as, "Oh really?", spoken with genuine interest, or "Tell me about it." "What happened then?" or "How did you feel when that happened?" let your children know that they have your attention, that you are taking time to deliberately listen.

5. Be Alert to Your Tone of Voice

Think back into your own childhood and recall the harsh voices of adults you tried to avoid. Remember a stern neighbor or a cranky aunt, people whose tones of voice made you shy away from associating with them. Then remember that special other adult who got down on one knee and looked you right in the eye as she gently asked how you were doing.

Your children understand your tone of voice. They are perhaps better listeners than we are when it comes to reading body language, facial expressions and tones of voice.

There are moments when we feel like yelling, but if we use restraint coupled with a gentle inquiry or response we will increase our effectiveness as listeners.

6. Build Trust

When your child does confide in you, it is a gesture of trust. The conversation should not be shared with outsiders. When your child learns that you told someone else the content of your discussion, he will be reluctant to share additional information with you in the future.

7. Become Shockproof

It is natural to give visceral gut-level responses when our children tell us things we believe they should not even know, or make statements that we cannot believe they are capable of saying. The parent's temptation is to give a "shock response," blurting out, "I don't ever want to hear you mention that again," or "Where did you ever get an idea like that?" Better, take a deep breath, think for a moment or two, and then in a tone of encouragement elicit the remainder of the information. If we truly want our children to talk to us, it becomes necessary for us to become shockproof.

✦

A family with three teenage daughters were discussing at the dinner table some of the daughters' views on human sexuality. One of the daughters asked an honest question: "Dad, what is circumcision?" Being relatively shockproof, the father was able to calmly answer the question, with no apparent dismay at the daughter's question.

9. Maintain Fairness in Your Conflicts

Have you ever heard parents say, "Do it because I said so," as they give orders to their children? There are times when a parent has the right to tell a child that she should do something just because the parent says so. However, when it comes to conflict between parents and children that are old enough to reason, the rules of conflict resolution need to become more two-sided. Of course, the parent can still lay down the law with no discussion and force the child to toe the line as long as the child lives in the same house. When that happens, however, the child is not being heard. Her questions are not being answered and the child begins to anticipate the time when she will no longer be under the same roof as the authoritarian parent.

Fairness means hearing all sides of the issue. Saying no to a child as an automatic response does not affirm the child's ability to make decisions. When we listen to our children, with a sincere desire to understand them, they develop a greater sense of self-esteem.

Ask yourself several questions when your child makes a request to do a particular thing: Is it harmful in any way? Does it go against our values? Can I truly trust my child in this situation? Remember, you are the parent. If, after hearing all the arguments, you still feel the request is not a good one, stand firm. Do not be afraid your children will not like you. That goes with the territory. There will be times when they do not like you. Your job is to give them stability, direction and a sense of values. Your job description, as a parent, does not include a promise that you will be liked by your children at all times.

When your children make solo decisions without consulting either parent and their choices go against the rules, do not panic. When you find out that your child tried a cigarette or a wine cooler or a can of beer, try not to act as though the world is coming to an end and that you have failed as a parent. Do take the time to sit down and express your disappointment about the decision your child has made. Enforce the consequences for breaking the rules and explain why they are being enforced. If your child persists in making anti-household decisions, in this case continuing to pursue the use of drugs in any form, the matter becomes much more serious and requires prompt attention. (At this point you may need professional outside help. The details of this assistance are beyond the scope of this book.)

10. Learn All You Can About Alcohol and Other Drugs

A recent national survey conducted by Weekly Reader Periodicals found that:

• Four out of ten sixth graders say there is pressure from other students to use alcohol or other drugs.

• Approximately thirty-five percent of fourth graders believe that drinking is "a big problem" for their age group.

These are elementary school children, fourth through sixth grade levels. They are already sensing peer pressure to use drugs. Much of their information about the nature of alcohol and other drugs they learn from other children. Some of that data is incorrect and misleading. Some of it is partially true. Some of it is correct.

You as a parent can provide correct information about alcohol and other drugs if you take the time to learn. Junior high school youngsters know a lot about drugs. Whether their schools have programs that attempt to teach the truth about drugs and alcohol or not, wise parents learn all they can about these substances.

What do we know about marijuana today? Is it an addictive drug? Does it make people dull or unmotivated? Is LSD a drug that children can find easily? What does it do? In what form is it sold? What are Sopors? Are they still available? What about speed or look-alikes; are they still around? Is alcohol all that bad for young people, in terms of what it can do to the body? Do you know about the truly addictive nature of cigarette-smoking?

You may be asked to answer questions like these. If you learn all you can about alcohol and other drugs, you are assured that your children will receive correct information from you about them.

Obviously, information alone is not the same as prevention. However, without correct information a child can more easily make an unwise choice about drugs. Armed with the facts a child can better refute the myths presented by her peers.

In addition to sharing facts with them, let your children know that you are against any use of these drugs, for any reason, and under any circumstances. If you know the facts, you are in a position to reinforce your own values and solidify your thinking regarding the use of drugs.

Investigate the many programs that promote a drug-free lifestyle. These efforts work to help your child clarify her values, to make good decisions and to solve problems without the use of drugs. Materials are inexpensive, and in many cases are free from the Federal Government (See Resources, page 123).

10

Things You Can Do In Your Community

In a large city high school in Florida, students used alcohol and other drugs freely. Parents served alcohol to their young people under the mistaken belief that all the other parents were doing the same and fearing that they would be the only "out-of-it" parents in the community. Several young people died in alcohol-related car crashes. Others made frequent trips to the local hospital emergency room for drug overdose treatment. Young people claimed the local drive-in restaurant as their hangout. On any given evening you could find them openly drinking beer outside their cars. Pot-smoking was only slightly less evident. This community is not unusual. What subsequently happened is, however.

One mother in this city, having seen her sixteen-year-old daughter come home drunk for the third time, decided she had had enough. She was angry at the out-of-control alcohol and other drug use among her daughter's friends. She felt guilty because she and her husband had been a part of the "open use" group of parents. She was sad because of the many young lives she saw being wasted. This mother was not a trained community organizer. Nor was she a prevention specialist. She was not a social worker or a psychologist. She was an angry mother who decided to try stemming the tide of adolescent drug use in her community.

The telephone became her weapon of choice. First she called all the other mothers and fathers she knew, asking their feelings about behavior in the community and expressing her own outrage. Some parents called her an alarmist; others declared that their young people were simply having a little fun. Still she persisted.

Eighteen months later the community's attitudes and norms had visibly changed. Underage drinking was no longer tolerated. Smoking was banned in and around the schools. Alcohol-free parties became the rule, not the exception.

Parents began to show up, unannounced, at weekend parties. Parents began to take chaperoning seriously and were eventually confronted with their own use of alcohol. Parents together decided upon acceptable guidelines for teenage parties, agreeing about reasonable curfews and appropriate behavior. For the first time these parents came together to take back the responsibility for their childrens' behavior and to assert their own values and norms within the community.

This is not a fairy tale. Some households ignore the community standards. A few young persons continue to do drugs. But despite that, alcohol and other drug use by high school students has dropped dramatically. One person's determination brought marked change to a community. Mothers Against Drunk Driving began in a community who wanted change, and grew into a movement that stretches across the United States and beyond. In many cases, change has come when one dedicated person declared, "I have had it! Enough is enough, and I am going to do something about it."

Do not be stymied by fears about how to organize or develop a master plan for your community. Consultants can offer advice at that stage. But experts have seldom *begun* these kinds of efforts. Instead, persons with ownership and commitment take charge of their own households, their streets and their schools so they become better places for children to grow.

1. Find the Facts about Drug and Alcohol Use

Each community has a unique set of characteristics—its ethnic make-up, its employment base, its traditions, its geography, the structure of its educational system. Each setting has different problems related to alcohol and other drug use and abuse. National statistics likely do not apply in every way to your particular locale. To do something positive about combatting drug abuse in your community, you must discover what the drug-use situation is there.

Start by contacting any of the following sources of information.

1. Teachers, Janitorial and Cafeteria Workers in Your School

They see your children every day. They are aware of students' tones and attitudes as they enter and leave the school building and classrooms, as they talk about and plan parties, as they work together on plays, sports and other extra-curricular activities.

2. School administrators

Ask the principal of the school where your children attend questions that will give you an idea of the nature and size of the problem: does your school allow high school students to stand outside at lunchtime and smoke cigarettes? Does your school system have a smoking room just for students? (Some schools do, much to the amazement of most parents.) Has your staff done alcohol and other drug use surveys? Could you obtain a copy of the results?

Be persistent. This is your community, your school and your neighborhood.

3. Health-care providers

This includes local mental health agencies, drug/alcohol treatment centers, as well as drug/alcohol prevention centers. How many drug/alcohol related cases are they seeing? What are the ages of the clients? What are the major drug-related problems they are seeing at the emergency clinic? Do they have any information regarding the size of the problem in your community? Do they know where you can get more data on the drug/alcohol problems in your community?

4. Law enforcement agencies

How many arrests are they making for driving under the influence of alcohol? What other drug use are they seeing? Do they have any figures they can give you? Do they know where else you can get specific information about drug and alcohol abuse in the community?

Some data you receive will be difficult to interpret; other data will be outdated. But do not lose sight of your goal: to document the fact that your community is not immune to the drug/alcohol abuse problems many people believe only happen elsewhere.

You are likely to learn that the major drug problem among young people is the use and abuse of alcohol. Find a way to talk with children, your own and others, and ask what they are seeing. Ask them about the activities students participate in on weekends. Discuss with other parents what their adolescents say about drug/alcohol use among fellow students.

2. Meet With Other Parents

Share the information you have obtained with parents whose interests and concerns overlap yours. A likely group are those with children of the same age as yours who attend the same school. You want to accomplish two things: encourage these parents to also work toward the prevention of drug use in your community, and to find out what they are seeing and hearing. Such gatherings become a relaxed forum for ascertaining the level of interest and commitment other parents have for working at these problems.

These meetings take time; it seems like almost too much time. Most of us want solutions that are easy to implement, inexpensive and proven to prevent drug abuse. There are no such programs. Alcohol and other drug prevention efforts require time, a great deal of energy and persistence. The problems did not develop quickly and they will not go away in a short period of time.

Meeting with other parents lays the groundwork for further outreach in the community. Drug prevention works best when grassroots persons clearly avow that they are fed up with out-of-control alcohol and other drug use by their children and youth.

You may believe that your children will never use drugs. You may feel sure that your parenting has been fairly strong and your children know where you stand.

Therefore, you may reason, why should I become involved? Why should I take the time and make the effort to work on drug prevention when I know my own children would never think of using drugs?

First, there are no guarantees that your child will never use drugs. We know that solid parenting reduces the chances that your child will use drugs, even when confronted with strong peer pressure. If, however, your child does use drugs, the network you have built with other parents will serve you well in times of crises. Second, the more dedicated you are to helping prevent drug abuse, in concert with other parents in your neighborhood, the greater the chance that there will be less drug use in the schools and in the community where your children are reared.

The benefits of working with and talking to other parents go beyond drug prevention. Such efforts help to build the sense of community that many older people remember from their childhoods. This is not romanticism, nor is it a wish for the good old days that drives this commitment to doing something positive. The motivation is simply to make your community a better place for all children and adults to live.

A national survey asked high school-aged students and recent graduates what they most wanted from life, excluding wealth. Their most often expressed wish was for a sense of community, a safe place to belong where each is known. Young people want to contribute to their community, and they are willing to join with adults if they believe they will be taken seriously.

3. Learn to Know People

Working at alcohol and other drug prevention has more to do with building community relationships than it does with storming the schools with information. Get to know the first and last names of all your childrens' friends. Make a point of talking with their parents on the telephone. Find out their feelings and observations about the schools and the community. Invite your children's friends to come to your home. Learn to recognize them on sight and to know something about their likes and dislikes, their joys and their disappointments. In other words, pay attention to the people in your own community.

Many of us, particularly we who live in large urban settings, do not know the names of our neighbors two doors away. Isolation and insulation flavor much of our society. Community involvement confronts this isolation directly. It begins to build a sense of belonging, a sense of extended family. Without forming this extended network, without involving other families, alcohol and other drug prevention efforts are doomed to failure. We need each other, our children need each other, and we cannot solve the drug problem if we hibernate, isolating ourselves from the rest of the world.

4. Fight Denial

Even as some families (especially parents) deny their child's drug problem in its early stages, so communities often refuse to acknowledge the presence of drug activity. Armed with the facts, you are in a position to serve as a resource, shedding light on the problem, clearly pointing out the details of what is really happening in the community. Tell the story to anyone who will listen. Show them the details and the statistics. More importantly, show them your concern and your caring for the children in your community. Facts and statistics alone will not convince others to join your cause.

As you inform and educate others regarding the variety of problems associated with drug use in your community, make a concerted effort to keep the information simple and straightforward. The use of overstatement or hysterical pleas will soon wear thin, and you will lose those people you most need. It is not hysterical to state the facts about an adolescent being killed in an alcohol-related car crash. It is not hysterical to inform people about the actual drug problem in your community. It is hysterical to exaggerate and inflate the data in order to make a point.

To fight community denial you will need to persist. School administrators may find it professionally embarrassing to admit there is a drug problem in their schools. They find it threatening if it is implied that they are not in control of the problem. Assure the principals and teachers that the problem was not created by them and they are not expected to solve it by themselves. Be certain to affirm the good job many of the school administrators are doing in giving your children quality education. Comment positively about the strong teachers your children have had. You are becoming involved to reinforce their work.

5. State Your Position

Parents, too, live with peer pressure. We are sometimes seduced into accepting a "live and let live" attitude rather than expressing what we believe, especially if it is different from the majority opinion. What do you really think about the use of alcohol? Is it all right for teenagers to drink alcoholic beverages in a "controlled" setting, where they will not be driving and where they will be protected?

Does your school have an alcohol/drug policy that is clearly stated and known by all the students and parents? What kind of policy would you develop if you were writing one for your child's school?

State your opinion, clearly and repeatedly, to anyone who will listen. We can arrive at basic agreements within our communities. Begin with a small group who share your intolerance for the use and abuse of alcohol and other drugs. Can you agree on the following statements which some communities are using as a starting point?

- Alcohol use is acceptable only for those of legal drinking age and only when the risk of adverse consequences is minimal.
- Prescription and over-the-counter drugs are used only for the purposes for which they were intended.
- Other abusable substances are used only for their intended purposes.
- Illegal drugs are not used at all.

If you are serious about these statements, there will be concrete results: no tolerance for cigarette machines being available to people under eighteen years of age, no tolerance for selling alcohol to minors, no tolerance for smoking in or around school property. There will be a concerted effort to discourage any use of alcohol at high school parties.

How far are you willing to go in making a statement? Are you fearful that other parents in the community will look upon you as a prohibitionist if you make bold declarations? Are you afraid that you may embarrass your children? Are you ready to be one of the first in your neighborhood to encourage other parents to prevent the use of alcohol at parties involving underage young people? Are you willing to meet with others in the community to develop a statement and then work toward the goals of implementing its concepts?

6. Join Anti-Drug Groups

Perhaps you are not a community organizer; perhaps you do not have the time or the inclination to gather information and call other parents together. Why not then join forces with organizations that are already in place?

Mothers Against Drunk Driving is a grassroots organization that has been solidly on the forefront of combating drunk driving. It is a single issue group, ably focusing attention on the devastation caused by drunk drivers. The rate of fatal car crashes in which a drinking driver was involved is dropping in the United States. Mothers Against Drunk Driving (MADD) has been key in raising awareness and promoting the seriousness of driving after drinking alcohol. MADD has chapters in nearly every city and welcomes volunteer helpers. (See the list of Resources at the back of this book for information about how to get in touch with MADD.)

Some schools have chapters of Students Against Driving Drunk (SADD), who welcome volunteer help from parents. You may want to assist in forming one of these groups in your school.

Your community may have a council on alcoholism or a school task force on drug/alcohol issues or a mental health board that deals with alcohol and other drug issues. Find the kind of organization that promotes values most congruent with your own. Research their effectiveness;

examine their literature. When you find an organization that suits your particular tastes, join it. Work actively for the group; commit yourself to being a part of the solution. It may be wise to limit your involvement to one or, at the most, two organizations and concentrate your efforts there, rather than becoming a ubiquitous board member around town. Keep in mind that if you have children, they are your first priority. Being on numerous committees, which take you out of the home on many evenings, does not contribute to strong family life.

7. Become Informed about Prevention Efforts

Discover what you can about the kinds of programs that work in communities similar to yours. Not all prevention efforts have had good success. Over the years there have been many approaches to prevention, from prohibition to the building of self-esteem. Even as families use different methods to prevent drug abuse, communities have varying approaches.

The mode you use likely depends upon the type of problem within your particular community. Underage drinking and the use of marijuana is one kind of problem. Crack dealers selling their wares in residential neighborhoods is a different situation requiring another approach.

Furthermore, prevention work must be consistent with the priorities, values, characteristics, political views and ways of communicating within a particular community. "The most effective approaches to prevent alcohol and other drug problems are comprehensive, coordinated, and include the entire social system," emphasizes the Office for Substance Abuse Prevention. While education can reinforce community values, it cannot function alone as an adequate prevention program.

What is the tack being taken by prevention efforts already in place in your community? Are the schools the main focus? Are churches and synagogues involved? Are law enforcement personnel being utilized? Is the major approach one of building self-esteem, teaching problem-solving skills, training to be able to say no, drug/alcohol education, or a combination of all these areas? Talk with the prevention people to learn about their goals and objectives. How will they measure their prevention efforts to know if they have produced a reduction in alcohol and other drug problems in the community?

When you have found answers to these questions, you will know better how to mesh your efforts with community programs already at work. Prevention plans that grow out of one individual's pet concerns, without being based on a proven model, are often doomed to failure. You will also increase your effectiveness by connecting with existing plans, provided they are well conceived and managed. For none of this do you need to be a prevention expert.

There are consulting firms that specialize in helping communities begin gathering and sharing information, as well as planning a prevention strategy. Many of these organizations will meet with you initially to help you evaluate your progress in building a concerted effort. If you want their further assistance in education and training, they can estimate the costs involved in that.

Think through these basic questions as you consider whether or not to engage a consulting group:

What are our needs at this moment in time?

- Information and education
- Training

- Development of a plan
- Ways to get started

How can this person(s) help us meet these needs?
How much will it cost?
How will their consulting fit into our overall plan?

Take great care in selecting a consultant. As alcohol and other drug prevention becomes a high priority for many communities, consulting firms have become plentiful, some more concerned with making a sizable profit than with meeting your needs.

Ask a firm which interests you for references from other communities that have used their services. Pursue those contacts.

Obtain a written bid for the exact costs that will be incurred by using their services. Be wary of hidden costs and expectations. For example, a firm may provide the necessary training and education materials, but fail to make it clear that your community will be required to spend a certain amount of money in advertising. Some groups stipulate that you sponsor a seminar, hiring only those people the consulting firm recommends. This can greatly inflate your cost.

Be sure to find out if they have a follow-up plan. Will they be available in one, two or three years from when you engage them? How long have they been in business? How successful have they been in the past? How do they measure success?

The process does not need to be long or laborious. It should instead be time-and money-saving. Too often enthusiastic community persons, eager to put together a sensible prevention program, charge ahead without enough knowledge, then become discouraged when it appears that few community leaders are supportive. Burn-out comes easily. By carefully planning in the beginning, each person can tackle particular tasks that fit the overall program.

You may be an interested volunteer, yet not in a position to bring in a consultant or outside resources. You may not have the time to develop a comprehensive plan. You can, however, attend community information and education sessions. Learn all you can about what is planned and already happening.

8. Volunteer

Every community has numerous organizations that are attempting to meet the needs of adolescents. Big Brothers and Big Sisters bring adults together with youth. Do prevention work by volunteering to have a Little Brother or a Little Sister. The close association of a young person with a caring adult is one of the best kept prevention secrets. One-to-one interaction is quality time, often seen by the child or adolescent as special: "This adult has chosen to be with me. This adult who does things with me cares about what happens to me. Maybe I am okay."

Other organizations welcome adult volunteers to work with adolescents. The local court system may have custody of a teenager who was caught stealing for the first time. The court needs caring adults to meet regularly with the youngster to provide guidance and encouragement. Childrens' homes wish for adults who will take individual children on afternoon excursions to the zoo or the park. Perhaps you know a single mother that dreams of an "uncle" or "aunt" for her young son or daughter. Volunteering as a dependable, regular, surrogate parent for a young person is one of the most effective drug prevention practices one can do. Not only are you a role model for that child or adolescent, you are showing your own children that you care about others.

Perhaps you like to work with groups of youth. The

Scouts and other such organizations are looking constantly for volunteers and welcome adult participation. Church and synagogue groups are eager for members who take a special interest in children and youth. Volunteer for the nursery. Volunteer to teach a Sabbath day class. Volunteer to go on a weekend retreat with the youth group. The list is endless; the point is simply stated: giving your precious volunteer time to children or adolescents is one of the most effective efforts you can make to promote healthy lifestyles.

9. Encourage Your Social Group to Get Involved

Are you involved with a church or synagogue? Are you active in a civic group such as the Rotarians or the Kiwanas? Do these social groups of yours work with drug prevention issues? Has your church or civic group had educational seminars to better inform its members? Maybe they are waiting for you to prod them into action.

Community groups work hard to be good citizens and promote good health.They are a prime audience for a series of lectures or debates on alcohol/drug-related issues. They may even be willing to look at some of the drug/alcohol problems within your community.

State and national organizations frequently produce or distribute prevention materials for their local chapters. Do some digging. You may discover information that would be useful to your group. Bring it to the leaders and ask that members become informed. Volunteer to take key responsibility within your church, synagogue or civic group for promoting drug/alcohol prevention.

10. Persist

Many of us, in our eagerness to begin, volunteer for too many responsibilities. We want to attack the drug problem head-on and we want to see results as soon as possible. Because this is a problem requiring persistence, take the long view. Choose a role in which you are comfortable working. Are you effective in dealing with children? Perhaps your efforts should be in that direction. Are you an organizer? If so, pitch in at the committee and community organization level. Do you have good communication skills? Consider being a speaker or presenter.

Whatever you choose to do in your community, remember that you are in it for the long haul. It may take years of effort until there is evidence that the younger generation is making decisions that are healthier than your generation made. But take heart. Consider the change that is happening in the United States regarding smoking. Young people are finally believing that smoking is a dangerous and addictive habit—and acting accordingly.

So consider what your contribution will be. Five areas of activity are crucial to a quality alcohol and other drug prevention program:

1. Share your practical skills for living. These most basic principles—decision making, communicating, taking of responsibility, managing money, solving problems, building relationships—are taught best by modeling. No matter your age or educational level, you have life skills that you can share with various groups of people.

2. Create alternatives. "Find positive and constructive means for addressing feelings of boredom, frustration, pain and powerlessness," urges the Office for Substance Abuse Prevention. Are you skilled at teaching young people how to have fun? What ideas do you have for alternative highs?

3. Select and adapt information that is appropriate for your community. Information is effective only if it is fitting for its audience.

4. Influence policy. Each community has its own set of family, school, governmental, community and media policies regarding alcohol and other drugs. Are you a letter writer? Are you articulate in expressing your views on policies in the community? Perhaps this is a place for you.

5. Help train and involve other people, including those who are role models in your community.

No matter what your educational background or your professional skills, you can contribute to the effort to undo the grip of alcohol and other drug abuse. Good information and teamwork are powerful forces.

Resources

Books for Adults

Arterburn, Steve and Jim Burns. *Drug Proof Your Kids.* Pamona, CA: Focus on the Family Publishing, Dobson Group, 1989.

Barun, Ken and Philip Bashe. *How to Keep the Children You Love* Off Drugs. New York: The Atlantic Monthly Press, 1988.

DuPont, Robert C., Jr., M.D. *Getting Tough on Gateway Drugs: A Guide for the Family.* Washington, DC: American Psychiatric Press, 1984.

Harrity, Anne Swany and Ann Brey Christensen. *Kids, Drugs, and Alcohol: A Parent's Guide to Prevention and Intervention.* Whitehall, VA: Betterway Publications, Inc., 1987.

Hutterian Brethren. *A Straight Word to Kids and Parents: Help for Teen Problems.* Ulster Park, NY: Plough Publishing House, 1987.

Jones, Dr. Ralph. *Straight Talk: Answers to Questions Young People Ask About Alcohol.* Bradenton, FL: Human Services Institute, 1988.

Perkins, William Mark and Nancy McMurtrie-Perkins. *Raising Drug-Free Kids in a Drug-Filled World.* Center City, MN: Hazelden Foundation, 1986.

Polson, Beth and Newton Miller, Ph.D. *Not My Kid: A Parent's Guide to Kids and Drugs.* New York: Arbor House, 1984.

Schwebel, Robert, Ph.D. *Saying No is Not Enough: Raising Children Who Make Decisions about Drugs and Alcohol.* New York: New Market Press, 1989.

Wilmes, David J. *Parenting for Prevention: How to Raise a Child to Say No to Alcohol/Drugs.* Minnesota: Johnson Institute Books, 1988.

Books for Elementary School Children

Alcohol Research Information Service. ***A Little More About Alcohol.*** Lansing, MI: ARIS, 1984.
1120 East Oakland Ave., Lansing, MI 48906. *Alcohol facts are explained through a cartoon character.* $0.75.

Cosby, William and Jim Willoughby. ***Buzzy's Rebound.*** Rockville, MD: National Clearinghouse for Alcohol and Drug Information, 1986.
P.O. Box 2345, Rockville, MD 20852. *This is a "Fat Albert" comic book that deals with the pressures on a new kid in town to try alcohol.* **Free.**

Hyppo, Marion H. and Jill M. Hastings. ***An Elephant in the Living Room:*** The Children's Book. Minneapolis: CompCare Publications, 1984.
Box 27777, Minneapolis, MN 55427. *Directed toward children in homes where alcoholism is present in parents.* $6.00.

Rattray, Jamie, et.al. ***Kids and Alcohol: Get High on Life.*** Pompano Beach, FL: Health Communications, Inc., 1984. 1721 Blount Rd., Suite 1, Pompano Beach, FL 33069. *This is a workbook designed for helping eleven- to fourteen-year-olds to make solid decisions and have good feelings about themselves.* $5.95.

Schwandt, Mary Kay. ***Kootch Talks About Alcoholism.*** Fargo, ND: Serenity Work, 1984.
1455 North University Drive, Fargo, ND 58102. *This 40-page color ing book features Kootch, the worm, and helps young children understand problems with drinking as well as alcoholism.* $3.00.

Seixas, Judith S. ***Alcohol: What It Is, What It Does.*** New York: Greenwillow Books, 1977.
105 Madison Ave., New York, NY 10016. *This is an easy-to-read, illustrated book on the use and abuse of beverage alcohol.* $5.95.

Weekly Reader Skills Books. ***Whiskers Says No to Drugs.*** Middletown, CT: Field Publications, 1987.
245 Long Hill Rd., Middletown, CT 06457. $1.50. *Contains interesting stories and follow-up activities for children in the six- to eight-year-olds range. It provides information and attitudinal situations to help children face peer pressure.*

Free Reading Materials for Adults

Write to:
National Clearinghouse for Alcohol and Drug Information
P.O. Box 2345
Rockville, MD 20852

Ask for:

- *Ten Steps to Help Your Child Say "No": A Parent's Guide,* 1986.
- *The Fact is. . .Hispanic Parents Can Help Their Children Avoid Alcohol and Other Drug Problems,* 1989.
- *The Fact is. . .You Can Prevent Alcohol and Other Drug Problems Among Elementary School Children,* 1988.
- *The Fact is. . .You Can Help Prevent Alcohol and Other Drug Use Among Secondary School Students,* 1989.
- *What Works: Schools Without Drugs, U.S. Department of Education, 1986* (revised in 1989).

For Free Materials,

including lending of videotapes on drugs, alcohol, and tobacco, contact:

Families in Action
National Drug Information Center
3845 North Druid Hills Rd.
Decatur, GA 30033
(404) 325-5799

National Clearinghouse for Alcohol
and Drug Information
P.O. Box 2345
Rockville, MD 20852
(301) 468-2600

National Council on Alcoholism
12 West 21st Street, Seventh Floor
New York, NY 10010
(212) 206-6770

National Institute on Drug Abuse Free-loan Collection
U.S. Department of Health and Human Services
Public Health Service
Alcohol, Drug Abuse and Mental Health Administration
Rockville, MD 20857
Order materials through:
Modern Talking Picture Service
Scheduling Center
5000 Park Street North
St. Petersburg, FL 33709
(813) 541-5763

Office for Substance Abuse Prevention
(ADAMHA/OSAP)
5600 Fishers Lane
Rockwall II Building
Rockville, MD 20857
(301) 443-0373

For Quick Connections to Nationwide Information Centers, contact:

(800) NCA-CALL	National Council on Alcoholism Information line.
(800) 241-7946	Parents' Resource Institute for Drug Education. (PRIDE).
(800) 662-HELP	National Institute on Drug Abuse (NIDA) Drug-Referral Hotline.
(800) COCAINE	Cocaine hotline for information and referral.
(800) 554-KIDS	National Federation of Parents for Drug-Free Youth.
(800) 258-2766	The Just Say No Foundation.
(800) 621-4000	National Adolescent Suicide Hotline.

For Local Information and Hotlines,

look in the Yellow Pages of the telephone book under:

- Alcoholism Information and Treatment Centers
- Drug Abuse and Addiction Information and Treatment
- Health Agencies
- Crisis Intervention Service
- Community Services

For Information on Parents' Groups, contact:

Mothers Against Drunk Driving (MADD)
669 Airport Freeway, Suite 310
Hurst, TX 76053
(817) 268-6233

National Asian Pacific American Families
Against Substance Abuse, Inc. (NAPAFASA)
6303 Friendship Court
Bethesda, MD 20817
(301) 530-0945

National Coalition of Hispanic Health
and Human Services Organizations. (COSSMHO)
1030 15th Street, NW, Suite 1053
Washington, DC 20005
(202) 371-2100

National Black Alcoholism Council, Inc.
53 West Jackson Blvd., Suite 828
Chicago, IL 60604
(312) 663-5780

Talking With Your Kids About Alcohol (TWYKAA)
Prevention Research Institute, Inc.
629 North Broadway, Suite 210
Lexington, KY 40508
(606) 254-9489

For Information about Childrens' Drug-Free Clubs and Organizations, contact:

The Just Say No Foundation
1777 North California Boulevard, Suite 200
Walnut Creek, CA 94596
(800) 258-2766; in CA, (415) 939-6666

Project LEAD
(Leadership, Experience and Development)
Quest International
537 Jones Rd
Granville, Oh 43023
(614) 587-2800

Students Against Driving Drunk (SADD)
P.O. Box 800
Marlboro, MA 01752
(617) 481-3568

Youth to Youth
700 Bryden Rd.
Columbus, OH 43215
(614) 224-4506